EPHES...
OUR SPIRITUAL
TREASURE

Exploring the Inexhaustible

Riches of Christ

By
Janet M. Magiera

LWM Publications
Light of the Word Ministry

Versions quoted are noted by abbreviations after the verse citation as follows:

AMP: Amplified Bible, The Lockman Foundation, 2015.

APNT: Aramaic Peshitta New Testament Translation, LWM Publications, 2006.

ESV: English Standard Version, Crossway, a publishing ministry of Good News Publishers, 2001.

KJV: King James Version of the English Bible, 1769 Blayney edition.

Lamsa: The Holy Bible from Ancient Eastern Manuscripts, A.J. Holman Company, 1968.

NASB: New American Standard Bible, The Lockman Foundation, 1977.

NET: The NET Bible, Biblical Studies Press, 1996.

NLT: New Living Translation, Tyndale House Publishers, 1996.

TPT: The Passion Translation, Passion & Fire Ministries, Inc., 2018.

LWM Publications, Light of the Word Ministry
6213 Lake Athabaska Place
San Diego CA 92119
www.lightofword.org

TABLE OF CONTENTS

INTRODUCTION

Ephesians has been a passion for me for as long as I have been a Christian. It is a book that I continually come back to study and find treasures inexhaustible. There have been so many times when specific verses and sections just "lived" for me so I wanted to share those insights and pour out the thoughts and love that God shared with me in the process of learning how to walk with him. Ephesians is the heart of the Father revealed to his children and his goal of having a family. It is the mystery of the Church and his hidden secret poured out on us as an intertwined body.

So many of the illustrations and metaphors of how to explain what the Church is are laid out in succinct fashion in that book! I believe that a lifetime is not nearly long enough to mine the treasures contained in six simple chapters. I have already written an entire book called *The Armor of Victory* on just the armor of God in Ephesians 6, and that doesn't even begin to explain all the depth that lies in that particular passage. My prayer is that this book will lead you to even greater "mining" than I have done. And my desire is that it would ignite your own search to explore the depth and the "inexhaustible riches of Christ."

I know many people have penned many words and many pages to try to capture the heart of Ephesians. I am indebted to many scholars who have helped me to understand particular verses and who have pointed the way to understand the overall outline of the book. I add this book to this great collection of study mainly because of the insight I have seen from the study of the Aramaic Peshitta New Testament. It is not intended to replace many other great works on the book of Ephesians but only to add to it in some fashion.

I present to you this approach to study this wonderful book of Ephesians with great joy in my heart that God, our wonderful Father, will "enlighten the eyes of your heart" and help you to see even more of his immense heart and love for each individual as well as everyone in the Church.

This study guide is written for the believer who desires to know more about the heart of the revelation of the one body of Christ as it is set forth in the book of Ephesians. The essays included in the book are the results of studies of the comparison of the Greek text and the Aramaic Peshitta text. The added understanding of the Aramaic meanings of words and phrases will "open the eyes of your hearts" and it is prayerfully given here for your continued building up and exhortation.

INTRODUCTION

The heart of what is available to learn and be understood in the book of Ephesians is simply summarized in the prayer in Ephesians 1.

Ephesians 1:17-19 APNT
that the God of our Lord Jesus Christ, the Father of glory, would give you the Spirit of wisdom and of revelation in his knowledge
and [that] the eyes of your hearts would be enlightened, so that you would know what is the hope of his calling and what is the wealth of the glory of his inheritance in the holy [ones]
and what is the abundance of the greatness of his power in us, in those who believe, according to the working of the might of his power.

The spiritual wisdom in Ephesians is to know:

1) Our calling—who we are in Christ
2) Our inheritance—our membership and place in the one body of Christ
3) Our power—how to live in the fulness of what we have been given

Our calling is described primarily in the first three chapters of Ephesians. Our inheritance is described in the last three chapters through 6:9. Our power is fully laid out in 6:10-18. This is the basic outline which is used in this study guide.

DEVOTIONAL BIBLE STUDY METHODS

The main purpose of this workbook on Ephesians is to use various methods of study in order to learn how to meditate on the Word of God and then apply it in our lives. These are devotional methods and even though there is some emphasis on the original languages, the study can be accomplished with only a Bible, this book and the Internet.

The devotional method gets its name from the word "devotion" which means "dedication, consecration, worship, and sincere attachment to a cause or person." The devotional method of Bible study increases our intimacy with God. It leads to worship and a deeper personal relationship with the Lord Jesus Christ. This method involves not only study of God's Word but also the application of its truths. It is not enough to just be "hearers of the Word." A person who is a hearer of the Word is one who studies God's Word but never applies the Word to his life.

What does it mean to meditate?

INTRODUCTION

Psalm 1:1-2 ESV
Blessed is the man who walks not in the counsel of the wicked, nor stands in the way of sinners, nor sits in the seat of scoffers;
but his delight is in the law of the LORD, and on his law he meditates day and night.

The godly man will make his delight in the righteous instruction of God, often translated "law" in the New Testament. What makes you happy? What gets you excited? Whatever that is shows what is important to you. If a person delights in something, you don't have to beg them to do it or to like it. They will do it all by themselves. You can measure your delight for the Word of God by how much you hunger for it.

Biblical meditation is essentially thought digestion or rumination. That is what a cow does when it chews its cud. Scriptural meditation is reading a passage over and over again, then thinking about it and concentrating on it in different ways until you have digested its meaning. Christian meditation means to fill the mind with God's instruction. It also includes verbalization, as well as brooding over, contemplating or mulling. Psalm 1 describes the man who delights and chooses to do this as a fruitful tree, planted in a garden.

In eastern meditation, the goal is to *empty* the mind. This is dangerous, because an empty mind may present an open invitation to deception or a demonic spirit. But in Christian meditation, the goal is to *fill* your mind with the Word of God. This can be done by carefully thinking about each word and phrase in many different ways.

The Hebrew word for "meditate" is *hagah*.... pronounced hagaaaaahhhhh, especially drawing out the "ah" sound. *Hagah* has a much deeper idea than just reading. Some definitions are to moan, growl, utter, muse, mutter, meditate, devise, plot and speak. It means pondering, musing, reading syllable by syllable, brooding over and then vocalizing the understanding of what is read and studied. When a hungry lion seeks food and then pounces on the prey, he then would *hagah*—growl and mutter to protect the kill if anything else tried to take it away and to emphasize his great delight in the food.

God exhorted Joshua after Moses died to meditate day and night, meaning all the time, AND to be careful to do what was written.

INTRODUCTION

Joshua 1:8 ESV
This Book of the Law shall not depart from your mouth, but you shall meditate on it day and night, so that you may be careful to do according to all that is written in it. For then you will make your way prosperous, and then you will have good success.

The Bible is like a door which leads into the presence of God. Behind that door are great spiritual treasures. But you must have the key to unlock the door or you will never be able to enter in and explore those treasures. The Bible reveals how to understand God's Word. It provides the keys to unlock the door to spiritual understanding. When we hunger to have that understanding, God's Word becomes not only our guide, but the way to live life fully.

The devotional methods used in this study guide are ways in which we can learn to meditate on a book, section, phrase, word or topic. The following is a list of methods used for each chapter. There is some overlap in the methods, and the titles are descriptive of the type of method and are not from a particular teacher or organization.

LESSON	METHOD
Overview	Encyclopedias and Bible dictionaries
1	Verse journaling and charts
2	Cultural understanding
3	Definitions of words and phrases
4	Word studies
5	Figures of speech
6	Asking questions, key words
7	Used before – quotations from OT
8	Context, word families
9	Prepositions and adverbs
10	Lexicons
11	Analogies and concepts
12	Application questions

There are two websites that I use primarily to access Bible references such as concordances, lexicons, translations and other resources. They are www.biblehub.com and www.biblestudytools.com. There are several others which can be utilized in a similar way, such as www.blueletterbible.org and www.biblegateway.com. E-Sword and The Word are excellent free software programs for Bible study. There are many commentaries and reference books available with those programs. These are the most commonly used references, but of course there are many more.

LESSON 1 ⊰ OVERVIEW OF EPHESIANS

When I first started studying the book of Ephesians, I did some background research on the history of the city of Ephesus and the worship of Diana there. This is an easy thing to do with the advent of modern technology. You can go to www.biblehub.com, find the topical section and search for Ephesus. Under this section, you can find several Bible dictionaries and encyclopedias in one place that all discuss the founding of the city and how the temple to Diana there was one of the seven wonders of the world. One of the simplest, yet most complete Bible dictionaries is *Easton's Bible Dictionary*. In this dictionary, we find this description of Ephesus:

> The capital of proconsular Asia, which was the western part of Asia Minor. It was colonized principally from Athens. In the time of the Romans it bore the title of "the first and greatest metropolis of Asia." It was distinguished for the Temple of Diana, who there had her chief shrine; and for its theatre, which was the largest in the world, capable of containing 50,000 spectators. It was, like all ancient theatres, open to the sky. Here were exhibited the fights of wild beasts and of men with beasts.

A far-reaching ministry happened in Ephesus with the apostle Paul. At first (around 51 A.D.) on his second missionary journey, God put up a roadblock to going to Asia and instead Paul traveled to Philippi and into Greece.

Acts 16:6 APNT
And they walked in the regions of Phrygia and of Galatia and the Holy Spirit hindered them from speaking the word of God in Asia.

But then after Paul had preached the gospel in Corinth for a year and a half and there met Priscilla and Aquila, he journeyed to Ephesus. This was on his way back to Antioch and he saw there a tremendous opportunity to preach the gospel.

Acts 18:18-19 APNT
And after Paul was there many days, he gave a farewell to the brothers and journeyed by sea to go to Syria. And Priscilla and Aquila went with him, after he had shaved his head in Cenchrea, because a vow was vowed by him.
And they arrived at Ephesus. And Paul entered the synagogue and was speaking with the Judeans.

Paul left Ephesus at that time, but promised to return. He left Priscilla and Aquila there to minister to the fledgling church. Later (around 54 A.D.) Paul came to Ephesus and there was a great outreach for at least two years and three months where "all they which dwelt in Asia heard the word of the Lord Jesus, both Jews and Greeks" (Acts 19:10).

There were many silversmiths who had prosperous businesses making statues of the goddess Diana in Ephesus and at the end of the two years, they put up a great opposition and caused a riot in the city. You can read all about it in Acts 19:23-41. Paul stayed longer in Ephesus than in any other city on his journeys. He was able to teach in the school of Tyrannus and the effectiveness of his ministry carried forward for the next 600 years.

During the time Paul was imprisoned in Rome (around 62 A.D.) he wrote four epistles which were delivered by four men. These letters are some of the most beautiful compositions of the Christian faith. These men were:

1. Epaphroditus (who was from Philippi) carried the epistle to the Philippians (Philippians 4:18)
2. Tychicus (who was from Ephesus) carried the epistle to the Ephesians (Ephesians 6:21)
3. Epaphras (who was from Colossae) carried the epistle to the Colossians (Colossians 4:12)
4. Onesimus (who was a runaway slave from Colossae) carried the epistle to Philemon who had been his master (Philemon 10)

All of these epistles present a complete picture of the mystery of Christ, the Church as the body of Christ and how it is to interact. There are many parallels in Colossians of sections in Ephesians, but there is more emphasis on Christ as the head of the body, rather than on the Church. Philippians presents practical examples of living in the Church and Philemon is also an example of how to be a Christian in a pagan society.

The core of the revelation of the mystery is masterfully presented in the book of Ephesians. Ruth Paxson, who was a missionary in China at the beginning of the 20th century, wrote several books on Ephesians and called it "the Grand Canyon of Scripture." She explained that in order to understand and appreciate the Grand Canyon, one cannot stand only on the rim and view it from above. But going down to explore the valley and really understand the magnitude of it from there is the best way. So it is with this wonderful book. We must see the varied colors in minute examination as well as in the overall scope.

Ephesians is a book that needs to be studied in detail to be able to find the treasures in it. Proverbs 2 shows us how to do this, as searching for silver. Silver is never found just on the surface, but when one follows a vein, then it will lead to the "mother lode" of understanding, knowledge and wisdom.

Proverbs 2:1-6 ESV
My son, if you receive my words and treasure up my commandments with you,
making your ear attentive to wisdom and inclining your heart to understanding;
yes, if you call out for insight and raise your voice for understanding,
if you seek it like silver and search for it as for hidden treasures,
then you will understand the fear of the LORD and find the knowledge of God.
For the LORD gives wisdom; from his mouth come knowledge and understanding;

GRACE AND PEACE

The greeting of the first two verses of the epistle are keynotes to the whole book. God's call to Paul as an apostle (a sent one with a message) by the will of God is to those who are born again and also faithful in Jesus Christ. This epistle is not for the Christian who only wants a nice feeling on Sunday. It is a challenge to any who want to live in peace and the grace of God and our Lord Jesus Christ.

Ephesians 1:1-2 APNT
Paul, an apostle of Jesus Christ, by the will of God, to those who are in Ephesus, holy [ones] and faithful [ones] in Jesus Christ:
Peace [be] with you and grace from God our Father and from our Lord Jesus Christ.

Peace comes from Christ himself. He is our peace. Christ brings us peace when we realize that he died for us and delivered us from sin and death and brought us into a relationship with God. Christ brings us peace when we realize that he gives the daily power to be an overcomer of anything negative in our lives. Christ brings a deeper peace when we realize that he has broken down all the divisions and barriers between God and man and between men.

Ephesians 2:13-14a ESV
But now in Christ Jesus you who once were far off have been brought near by the blood of Christ.
For he himself is our peace ....

Grace is probably the most meaningful word in this epistle. It means all the favors and gifts of God's goodness. Everything good and beneficial that God has given and does give to us is wrapped up in the idea of grace. In Aramaic, the root verb of the word for grace means "to be good." Grace is the favor or goodness of God showered on men who have neither earned it nor deserved it.

Ephesians 2:8-9 APNT
For by his grace we were redeemed by faith and this was not from yourselves, but is the gift of God,
not from works, so that no one would boast.

Can you imagine what it was like when this letter was first read to the church at Ephesus? It had been a number of years since they had seen Paul and they had heard that he was in prison and of course were concerned about that. Tychicus comes with the letter from him and news about Paul and it must have provided great comfort to them. Now they have an awe-inspiring letter to read repeatedly and to use to "grow up into Christ" (Ephesians 4:14-15). We have this same privilege because this book has been preserved through the centuries to bring this same peace and grace to us today.

LESSON 2 ✠ ALL SPIRITUAL BLESSINGS IN CHRIST

KEY VERSE

Ephesians 1:3 KJV
Blessed be the God and Father of our Lord Jesus Christ, who hath blessed us with all spiritual blessings in heavenly places in Christ:

In this short sentence, we are escorted onto the threshold of the house of riches that we have been given in Christ. There we are given the key to this house of spiritual treasures and invited in to explore it. A saint is one who has left the sphere of the natural and become a possessor of a heaven-born nature, so he must have heaven-sent supplies to nourish and develop it. These are the spiritual blessings in heavenly places it is talking about in this verse. It does not mean that we are in heaven right now, but the heavenly privileges and power that belong to Christ right now as the resurrected Lord are given to us so that we may live on a heavenly plane even though still actually physically on the earth. Ruth Paxson puts it this way:

> Living in a non-spiritual world, he needs a spiritual atmosphere in which to breathe; spiritual food to eat; spiritual garments to wear; spiritual companions with whom to fellowship; spiritual exercise to keep fit and strong; spiritual strength to endure suffering and afflictions; spiritual weapons with which to war.[1]

These are not all of the kinds of blessings, only a few. All spiritual blessings is literally all blessings of the Spirit or EVERY blessing of the Spirit. This whole chapter is filled with blessings of what we have in Christ. In fact, the whole book of Ephesians is a masterful summation of our new life in Christ. The verb "blessed" in its simplest meaning is "to bow down" or "to bend the knees." In fact, the word knee also comes from this verb. The verb also means "to bend the knee to bring a gift." We needed to become children of God and receive salvation by humbling ourselves to God. Then he bestowed his blessing on us—filling us with his Spirit. We had to bow down and accept what the Lord Jesus had done for us in order to receive God's blessings. Now we in turn bless God. God is blessed and He HAS blessed us and all of those blessings are OURS.

---

[1] Paxson, Ruth, *The Wealth, Walk and Warfare of the Christian*, p. 26.

EXERCISE

In order to get this deep into our hearts before we go on, this is one way to let the individual phrases of this verse become deeply meaningful.

1. Recite the verse out loud.
2. Read the verse with emphasis on each phrase and see how it changes the meaning. (Examples: BLESSED BE… ALL SPIRITUAL BLESSINGS… IN CHRIST…)
3. Look up three other translations of the verse and write down your favorite one.

Other version:

_____

_____

IN CHRIST

The next part of this lesson is about the words "in Christ." This is the key to heaven's treasury and the opening of our understanding of its wealth. First, we will look at what the word "Christ" means.

The word Christ means simply, "the anointed one." In Hebrew it is spelled *Mashiach* and in Aramaic *Meshikha* and we derive the English word Messiah from these. But what does anoint mean? In both Hebrew and Aramaic, the verb anoint means to rub on, pour on, smear or saturate and is spelled *mashach* in Hebrew and *meshakh* in Aramaic.

Acts 10:38 APNT
concerning Jesus, who was from Nazareth, whom God anointed [meshakh] with the Holy Spirit and with power. And this is he who traveled around and healed those who were oppressed by the Evil [one], because God was with him.

We can see several things right away without knowing anything about the word "anointed." God anointed Jesus with Holy Spirit and with power. The result was healing and deliverance from the oppression of the Evil One. Then it says *"because God was with him."* Let's keep these things in mind while we are looking at the meaning of anoint.

Psalm 133 is the shortest Psalm and it describes how when Aaron was anointed as the high priest for Israel when the tabernacle was first started, it saturated him.

LESSON 2 ✠ ALL SPIRITUAL BLESSINGS IN CHRIST

Psalm 133:2-3 ESV
It is like the precious oil on the head, running down on the beard, on the beard of Aaron, running down on the collar of his robes!
It is like the dew of Hermon, which falls on the mountains of Zion! For there the LORD has commanded the blessing, life forevermore.

When Aaron was anointed, as well as other prophets, kings and priests in the Old Testament, it was not just a few drops sprinkled on his head. It poured down all the way past his beard to his robes. He was saturated! When I was in Israel, we rode a cable car up to the top of Mount Hermon in the northern part of Israel. It is the highest mountain in the area. There was so much dew that we were soaked by the time we got up to the top! That is why the dew of Hermon is an apropos analogy to anointing.

Jesus was anointed with Holy Spirit and it saturated him. Men and women in the Old Testament were given the Spirit as a gift to them, but there were different amounts for different people. Jesus, the Anointed One, had the fullest amount of Spirit ever given to any person before.

John 3:34 ESV
For he whom God has sent utters the words of God, for he gives the Spirit without measure.

Now we come to see a word which will tie all the understanding together. That is the word "measure." The verb *meshakh* in Aramaic is a homonym. That means it has two meanings depending on the context of the use. It is similar to our English word "bank." Depending on the context, we understand a bank to be either place where money is or the edge of a river. The first meaning of the verb is "to saturate, pour," but the second meaning is "to measure." Since all the nouns formed from this root are related to the verb, some nouns also mean measure. The noun "measure" in Aramaic is *meshukhtha*. See how close it is to *meshikha*, or Christ? The anointing is the full measure of the Spirit that was in Jesus, the Anointed One. This becomes clear in Ephesians 4.

Ephesians 4:7 APNT
Now to each one of us is given grace according to the measure [meshukhtha] of the gift of Christ [meshikha].

LESSON 2 ⬙ ALL SPIRITUAL BLESSINGS IN CHRIST

Ephesians 4:13 APNT
until we all become one in the faith and in the knowledge of the Son of God and one mature man, in the measure [meshukhtha] of the standing of the fullness of Christ [meshikha].

God not only anointed Jesus with the full amount of Spirit, but then he gave it to us as a gift. We have the full measure of the anointing that was on Jesus! Our connecting point is that we all have the same gift. It is like a measuring cup that is full to the brim. We are all bonded together by the gift of the Holy Spirit, no matter where we are or how differently we may be in utilizing it. We have the same measure of the Spirit that was in Christ. That means we can walk like he walked: with his love, with his compassion, with his peace and with the same confidence that he had as God's Son. Think about how he manifested love and compassion toward the people he was ministering to and with, and know that you have that same gift!

2 Corinthians 1:21-22 ESV
And it is God who establishes us with you in Christ, and has anointed [meshakh] us, and who has also put his seal on us and given us his Spirit in our hearts as a guarantee.

What is the purpose of the anointing? To do the same works that Jesus did with power and authority!! Heal the sick, raise the dead, and proclaim liberty to the captives! The same power that God anointed (saturated) Jesus with is OURS. Now we know what it is to have "Christ in us, the hope of glory" (Colossians 1:27). It is having the full measure of the Spirit of God in Jesus Christ.

In the Messiah, who is the Christ, the risen resurrected Lord, we have some wonderful things. To be "in" something means to belong to that "something." The "in crowd" is a good example of a slang usage of the word "in," If you are "in" something, you are not outside of it. Also, you have some specific qualities or characteristics which qualify you to be in the group. Once you're "in," then you can participate in all the activities of those who are included in that group.

The phrase "in Christ" in Ephesians describes our "in crowd" and what characteristics we have in that group because of what Christ accomplished and who he is. The first chapter of Ephesians is filled with the phrases, "in Christ," "in whom," "in him," "in the beloved." In fact, these phrases are used 10 times in the Aramaic translation in the first 14 verses.

The Aramaic way of writing a prepositional phrase like "in Christ" is to take the word for Christ, *meshikha,* and then add the letter b, or *beth,* in front of the word. The phrase "in Christ" would be written *b'meshikha*, and "in him" is *b'ha*, and "in the beloved" is *b'khuva.*

EXERCISE

Let's look at some of the places where *beth* is attached to the noun in Ephesians 1:3-14. First, I want you to take a highlighter and, on the Aramaic translation on the following page, highlight every place you see "in" referring to Christ and see if you can find all 10 times. (If you prefer to use King James and study the Greek word *en* with Christ or him, there are 11 times—an additional one is in verse 6.)

Now go back and see the highlighted verses and make a list of all the phrases of what we have in Christ with the verse notation so you can go back and review them later.

VERSE	BLESSINGS
3	
4	
5	
7	
9	
10	
11	
12	
13	
13	

LESSON 2 ✦ ALL SPIRITUAL BLESSINGS IN CHRIST

When we first trusted in Christ, we received the "saturation" of the full measure of the Spirit and with it all spiritual blessings. God chose us and made us his sons!

Ephesians 1:3-14 APNT

3 Blessed be God, the Father of our Lord Jesus Christ, who has blessed us with all spiritual blessings in heaven in Christ,

4 even as he chose us beforehand in him, from before the foundations of the world, that we should be holy [ones] and without blemish before him. And in love, he marked us out beforehand for himself

5 and he adopted us in Jesus Christ, as was pleasing to his will,

6 that the glory of his grace would be glorified, which he has poured on us by way of his beloved [one],

7 in whom we have redemption and remission of sins by his blood, according to the wealth of his grace,

8 which he caused to abound in us with all wisdom and with all understanding.

9 And he made known to us the mystery of his will that he had determined beforehand to accomplish in him,

10 in the administration of the fullness of times, that everything that is in heaven and in earth should be made new again in Christ.

11 And we were chosen in him, even as he marked us out beforehand and he desired, he who performs everything according to the purpose of his will,

12 that we, those who first trusted in Christ, should be for the esteem of his magnificence.

13 In him also, you heard the word of truthfulness, which is the gospel of your life, and in him, you believed and you were sealed with the Holy Spirit that was promised,

14 which is the guarantee of our inheritance to the redemption of those who have life and to the glory of his honor.

FURTHER STUDY AND DISCUSSION

1. What is the blessing that strikes you the most from these verses?

2. What part of verses 3-14 would you like to learn more about?

3. What is another example of being "saturated"?

LESSON 3 ♦ WHAT'S SO SPECIAL ABOUT US?

<u>EXERCISE</u>

Whenever an article or written story appears in a newspaper or magazine, most often the pronouns used are in the third person, using "he" or "they." When "we" is used, the story is an eyewitness account of a specific group of people which includes the writer and those who belong to the group. "We" or "us" are thus inclusive terms and can only be used when one belongs to a group. Something definitive sets the "we" and "us" apart from those outside of the group.

Throughout the book of Ephesians, there are key sections which are emphasized by the use of "we" and "us." Specific phrases describe the group to which "us" refers and what that group has that makes it unique and special. The group is the Church of the one body and it has had some very definite and wonderful things given to it in Christ Jesus. This study is about "us" and what is so special about "us."

In Aramaic, the pronoun "us" can be attached as a suffix to a verb or to a preposition. These are the places that are noted in the verses in this study. Now, since "you" most likely are a member of the one body of Christ (and if not, can be so by believing Romans 10:9-10) "you" can now include yourself in the "us" of the verses from Ephesians and think about how special you are. Go back to the previous lesson and put a colored box around every place you find the word "us." There are 9 uses in the first 14 verses, because in verse 7, the phrase "we have" in Aramaic is literally "there is to us."

Now I want to spend a good portion of the time in this lesson meditating on what it means to be adopted as sons.

<u>KEY VERSE</u>

Ephesians 1:5 KJV
Having predestinated us unto the adoption of children by Jesus Christ to himself, according to the good pleasure of his will,

There are three different cultures that need to be reviewed in order to understand how this phrase in Ephesians 1:5 should be translated. In the Jewish culture, adoption was secondary to being born as a natural son. There are incidents of adoption in the Old Testament. For example, Abraham adopted his steward, Eliezer, as his heir when he had no children (Genesis 15:2-3). But emphasis was normally on the firstborn son, and since the firstborn son received a double portion of the inheritance, this was very important.

The same emphasis is true in our culture. If one is adopted, there is a perception that the real father was somehow not responsible or willing to care for the child. Being a natural child is considered to be much more important than to be adopted. In fact, that is why we call being saved as being "born again" as it is described in 1 Peter and John 3.

1 Peter 1:23 APNT
Like a man, you were born anew, not of seed that is corruptible, but of that which is not corruptible, by the living word of God that stands forever.

To be born anew literally means to be "born from above" or born again. Because being born into a family is so important in our estimation, this phrase is used more often to describe sonship than adoption.

However, in the Greek and Roman cultures, adoption was more important than being a natural son. An example is in the succession of the Caesars. More often than not, the successor was an adopted son rather than the natural son. Augustus Caesar was adopted by his uncle Julius Caesar Gaius Octavius and became Gaius Julius Caesar Octavianus. Even his name was changed to reflect his new status as the son of Julius Caesar.

Perhaps you have seen the movie, Ben Hur. Judah Ben Hur rescued a naval commander, Quintus Arrius, and was adopted by him, changing his status from being a slave to a son. All the rights and privileges of being a Roman citizen belonged to him after the adoption.

Now we can begin to see that there are significant reasons why the word "adoption" is used in Ephesians 1:5, as well as in Romans 8:15 and Galatians 4:5. There are five main points that are specific to our adoption with God as our Father.

1. We are purchased.

Galatians 4:4-5 KJV
But when the fulness of the time was come, God sent forth his Son, made of a woman, made under the law,
To redeem them that were under the law, that we might receive the adoption of sons.

The word "adoption" is actually an idiom that literally means "placed as sons." It could be translated sonship but it is better to leave it as the idiom. The word "redeem" in these verses means to purchase or buy, to buy up for oneself. There was a price that God paid for the adoption—the death of his only begotten Son.

2.   We have received a new name.

Galatians 4:6 APNT
And now that you are sons, God sent into your hearts the Spirit of his Son that calls, "Father, our Father."

Now our new name is no longer "slave," but "son." Galatians 4:3 says that we were in "bondage under the elements of the world." The slave has been made a son, just as in the story of Ben Hur. That is the reason Galatians 4:6 says that now we can call God our Father and say, "Abba, Father."

Albert Barnes' *Notes on the Bible* denotes that servants could not use the title of Abba. It is also denoted in the Babylonian *Gemara*, a Jewish work, that it was not permitted for slaves to use the title of Abba in addressing the master of the family to which they belonged. If so, then the language which Christians are here represented as using is the language of freemen, and denotes that they are not under the servitude of sin.

3.   All debts are cancelled.

Romans 8:15 APNT
For you have not received the spirit of bondage again to fear, but you have received the Spirit of adoption by which we call, "Father, our Father."

In the Roman culture, not only would the adopted man receive a new name, but all debts would be cancelled upon the adoption. Any ramifications of the bondage that we had to sin is cancelled. This is explained in many other passages in the epistles, including this great illustration in Colossians:

Colossians 2:14 APNT
And he has blotted out, by his commandments, the handwriting of our debts that was against us and he took it from the middle and fastened it to his cross.

4. We are sealed with the Holy Spirit.

Ephesians 1:13-14 APNT
In him also, you heard the word of truthfulness, which is the gospel of your life, and in him, you believed and you were sealed with the Holy Spirit that was promised, which is the guarantee of our inheritance to the redemption of those who have life and to the glory of his honor.

Ephesians 1:3 says that we have all spiritual blessings. Every kind of blessing of the Spirit is ours! We were also given the seal of the Spirit to use in all of our everyday life. When something is sealed, it shows the sign of its authenticity. Seals were used in many cultures to guarantee that a letter or contract was genuine. The seal in the Roman culture allowed a person to transact any kind of business and it would be backed up by everything that the father owned. The seal is not only a "token" of our inheritance, but it is to be used each and every day.

Ephesians 4:30 APNT
And you should not grieve the sanctified Spirit of God, by whom you were sealed until the day of redemption.

We have been sealed with God's Spirit and it guarantees that we will receive our full inheritance. This sealing is a guarantee that we will have a full redemption from death to life and that we will also receive new bodies fashioned like Jesus' glorious resurrected body. The Hebrew word for "sealed" was used in the record of Judah giving his seal to Tamar as a pledge (Genesis 38:17-20). It was like a "credit card" and Judah exchanged it for a promise to take care of Tamar. God has given us a down payment (or use of his credit card) by the gift of the Spirit to continually remind us that the full redemption is coming in the future.

5. We have an inheritance.

Romans 8:23 APNT
And they are not alone, but we also who have the first[fruit] of the Spirit groan within ourselves and we wait for the adoption and the redemption of our bodies,

Our full inheritance will be received when our physical bodies are also changed to become like Christ's resurrected body. And we will receive the full inheritance that Jesus Christ has now. Jesus Christ is the firstborn son and normally would get the largest portion and the rest would be divided up among the sons. However, God has made us "joint-heirs" with Jesus Christ. That means we share equally in everything that he has, not just a portion!

Romans 8:17 APNT
And if [we are] sons, [then] also heirs, heirs of God and fellow-heirs of Jesus Christ, that if we suffer with him, we will also be glorified with him.

Adoption had two portions: a private and then a public ceremony. The public ceremony was a formal declaration that this person was now a son. Freeman, in *Bible Manners and Customs,* describes this ceremony like this:

> Among the Romans there were two parts to the act of adoption: one a private arrangement between the parties, and the other a formal public declaration of the fact. It is thought by some that the former is referred to in this verse [Rom 8:15], and the latter in verse 23, where the apostle speaks of "waiting for the adoption." The servant has been adopted privately, but he is "waiting" for a formal public declaration of the fact.

Now we have begun to see that adoption is a much bigger concept than at first it appears to be. We are purchased, we have a new name, all debts are cancelled, we have been sealed and we will receive the full inheritance of Jesus Christ!

EXERCISE

After this section in Ephesians 1, the pronouns change to "you" and "I" for a while until 1:19 where the "us" begins again, emphasizing we who believe. Please go through the following section and make another colored box around all of the uses you can find of the words "we" and "us."

LESSON 3 ⬥ WHAT'S SO SPECIAL ABOUT US?

Ephesians 2:1-10 APNT

1 And [God is filling] even you who were dead in your sins and in your transgressions,

2 in which you had walked previously, according to the worldliness of this world and according to the will of the chief authority of the air and of that spirit that operates in the sons of disobedience.

3 We also were occupied in those deeds previously, in the desires of our flesh, and we were doing the will of our flesh and of our mind and we were the sons of wrath [as] fully as the rest.

4 But God, who is rich in his mercies, because of his great love [with] which he loved us,

5 while we were dead in our sins, gave us life with Christ and, by his grace, redeemed us

6 and raised us with him and seated us with him in heaven in Jesus Christ,

7 so that he could show to the ages that are coming the greatness of the wealth of his grace and his goodness that is to us in Jesus Christ.

8 For by his grace we were redeemed by faith and this was not from yourselves, but is the gift of God,

9 not from works, so that no one would boast.

10 For we [are] his own creation, who are created in Jesus Christ for good works, those [works] which God prepared previously that we should walk in.

After Ephesians 2:10, the rest of the book is primarily written in the first person "I" or second person, "you." But there are several key verses where abruptly the pronouns change to "we" and "us" for emphasis on the one body at that point. They bring out something very specific to note about the "us." In the section of Ephesians 2:11-21, the one verse is Ephesians 2:18 which is written with "we": "because in him we both have access by one Spirit unto the Father." Again, the literal rendering in Aramaic of "we have" is "there is to us." To us there is access by one Spirit to the Father. That is the heart of the sonship explained!

Which part of this chapter blessed you the most? Why?

_____

_____

_____

_____

FURTHER STUDY AND DISCUSSION

1. Have you known someone who was adopted? How do they feel about that and why?

2. What are some things that are included in our inheritance?

3. What are some examples of an "earnest" or "guarantee?"

LESSON 4 ⬥ TO THE PRAISE OF HIS GLORY

In this lesson, we will explore with you from both the Greek and Aramaic about the three times in chapter one it says, "to the praise of his glory." The reason I want to share from both languages is that each language contributes to the overall understanding. And the context then supplies the emphasis of each phrase.

There are three key words in Greek in verse six in the phrase "to the praise of the glory of his grace." These are *epainos*, *doxa* and *charis*. *Epainos* is commendation or praise and it is only used of man to God. The idea is that the one being praised is worthy of special recognition. God the Father (verse 3) blessed us with all spiritual blessings and he gave all these wonderful things to us. That is worthy of special recognition by us back up to him. He chose us so that we could be holy and without spot or blame. That blessing deserves recognition. What does it recognize? It is praise or recognition for the "glory of his grace."

Glory is *doxa*, which is the reflective representation of something, showing power, splendor or honor. Grace is *charis,* an unmerited gift or divine favor. Both of these words are full of weight and significance. But the most important thing to note is the emphasis of the phrase. It is a figure of speech where the genitive of possession (grace's) is put as a prepositional phrase (of his grace). What that emphasizes is the word "grace." It could be translated his glorious grace, but saying it with this figure makes it mean, glory of his GRACE. Thus, what is being commended or praised is God's grace. His divine favor is totally worthy of recognition of the highest amount of praise.

In the Greek culture, when a man who owned slaves died and, in his will, gave the slaves their freedom, they would put on a cap of liberty to show that they were now free. At the funeral and afterward, they would parade in the town and streets telling all that their master was so great—he had set them free. That custom is described as being "to the praise of his glory." In other words, they were showing the greatness and splendor of the master because he had set them free. God has certainly set us free, so we can be to the praise of his glory. We are recognizing the greatness and splendor of our God, because of what he has given us in Christ.

In Aramaic, there are three different phrases using separate words for the three uses of "to the praise of his glory" in Ephesians 1. Let's look at them one at a time. Usually in the comparison of the two languages, there are matching words with some variations, and one can say this Aramaic word lines up with *epainos*, this one with *doxa*, etc. In this case, the Aramaic has very specific words in specific order. This is a puzzle to know why they are different. That is what we will see and it will add to our understanding.

KEY VERSE 1

Ephesians 1:6 KJV
To the praise of the glory of his grace, wherein he hath made us accepted in the beloved.

Ephesians 1:6 APNT
that the glory of his grace would be glorified, which he has poured on us by way of his beloved [one],

As you can see, "made us accepted" in the King James Version is not in Aramaic, but instead there is a beautiful picture of grace being poured out upon us. "The glory of his grace would be glorified" is a figure of speech, *polyptoton*, where the same root is used in different forms. In this case, first the noun is used and then the verb. You could also say, "the magnitude of his grace may be magnified" or "greatness of his grace may be aggrandized." This Aramaic word for "glory" is the simple word and lines up most of the time with *doxa*. This confirms what we have seen before, that the emphasis of the first eight verses is all GRACE. That is what we glorify because he poured it out upon us in Christ!

What is your own description of grace? Is anything added to it because of understanding verses 3-8?

_____
_____
_____

The next use of the phrase "to the praise of his glory" is in verse 11, but please read verses 9-12 to understand the context. You could also read this section in several different translations besides the Aramaic Peshitta.

KEY VERSE 2

Ephesians 1:12 KJV
That we should be to the praise of his glory, who first trusted in Christ.

Ephesians 1:12 APNT
that we, those who first trusted in Christ, should be for the esteem of his magnificence.

The Aramaic translation of "to the praise of his glory" in verse 12 is "for the esteem of his magnificence." Esteem is *hedra*, and can mean excellency. It is from an Aramaic root, meaning "to be adorned." Magnificence is an intensified word for glory, not the simple word, thus the translation. It could be absolute glory or splendor.

1 Corinthians 2:7-8 says that if Satan had known that the same power Jesus Christ has would be in every believer, he never would have crucified Jesus Christ. We are to the praise of his glory, to the esteem of his magnificence, because we show in the mystery of Christ the glorious will and wisdom of God.

Write out your thoughts and insights. How is God magnificent to you?
_____
_____
_____
_____
_____

KEY VERSE 3

Ephesians 1:14 KJV
Which is the earnest of our inheritance until the redemption of the purchased possession, unto the praise of his glory.

Ephesians 1:14 APNT
which is the guarantee of our inheritance to the redemption of those who have life and to the glory of his honor.

The last time the phrase is used is in verse 14, but first go back and read verse 13. We were sealed with the gift of Holy Spirit as we learned in the last lesson. This is to the praise of his glory! The Aramaic translation is to the "glory of his honor." Glory is the basic word for splendor again, but here it is used instead of praise. The word honor comes from the Aramaic verb meaning "to be heavy, or have weight." If something or someone has honor, he is heavy, he has value or weight.

All the power of that Spirit or down payment of our inheritance is ours to manifest and use including all nine manifestations, some of which are: receiving revelation, gifts of healings, discerning of spirits, as well as the fruit of the Spirit which is love joy, peace, etc. But here is how it works: God is Holy (Leviticus 20:26) and God is Spirit (John 4:24). Then on the day of Pentecost he gave the gift which is Holy and which is Spirit. He gave what he is! So every time we use that gift and show it forth we show the value or honor of God.

What is the honor or value that God has for you personally?

_____

_____

_____

EXERCISE

Pick three key words from this lesson and go online and look up basic definitions of the Greek words and fill in the chart. (Hint: glory, grace, accepted, praise, token).

WORD	GREEK	STRONG'S #	DEFINITION

FURTHER STUDY AND DISCUSSION

1) What kinds of things bring praise to God?

2) What is your understanding of glory in your own words?

3) Grace is a prominent theme in Ephesians. Was there grace in the Old Testament too?

LESSON 5 ✥ WHAT GOD DID BEFOREHAND

The first three chapters of Ephesians set the stage for knowing and experiencing the hope of our calling and the riches of the glory of our inheritance (Ephesians 1:18-19).

There is a small word in Aramaic, *qedam*, which means "beforehand." This word is used in combination with other verbs as an adverb to tell the time in which an action took place. It is very revealing to see these combinations of what God did beforehand in light of our calling. Four of the uses of *qedam* are in the first chapter of Ephesians.

<u>KEY VERSE</u>

Ephesians 1:4 APNT
even as he chose us beforehand in him, from before the foundations of the world, that we should be holy [ones] and without blemish before him. And in love, he marked us out beforehand for himself

God chose us beforehand. The exact time of this is further clarified by the next phrase: before the foundations of the world. Before the founding of the world, God chose us. That is a remarkable truth. We ought to be jumping up and down and shouting "Glory, hallelujah!" God in his wisdom knew that we would believe so he knew that when he called, we would answer the call. He had it all set up and knew that we would be saints, "holy [ones]," and would be able to stand before him without blemish. Before God created the heavens and the earth, he had us in mind.

The verb for "marked out" is the Aramaic word, *reshem*, which means to engrave, mark, inscribe. It is used in the Peshitta Old Testament in Isaiah 49:16, where God "engraved us on the palms of his hands." We were inscribed on God's hands beforehand—before the foundation of the world! How did he do this? By his foreknowledge, he already knew that we would believe by our freedom of will and would become a part of his family.

To be "marked out" means to be engraved like a tattoo or an etching on stone. I had a friend who wanted to erase a tattoo and it was a very lengthy and painful process to get it to even fade. The engraving of a tattoo is very permanent. Another example of engraving is on stone. Archaeologists are finding words written in stone from the Near East, when most other ways of writing have long disintegrated. One use of this verb "marked out" is in Romans 8:29: "he marked them out with the likeness of the image of his Son."

The word for "marked out" is *proorizo* in Greek and means "to appoint before" or "to mark off or to set off the boundaries of something." We get the English word "horizon" from the basic Greek verb. Just like God marked out the horizon for the separation between earth and heaven, he marked out the place where we would be in the future. He marked the boundary of our being adopted as sons of God, made just like Christ and conformed to his very likeness and image. The King James Version translates this as "predestined." It has been taught in theology about "predestination" that we have no choice about it. But our free will is never violated by God. It is only that God is all-knowing so he knows what we will choose. And he knew this before the foundations of the world!

The next use of *qedam* in Ephesians 1 shows more about God's knowledge beforehand.

Ephesians 1:9-10 APNT
And he has made known to us the mystery of his will, which he had determined beforehand to accomplish in him
in the administration of the fullness of times, that everything that is in heaven and in earth should be made new again in Christ.

God set or determined beforehand, before the foundation of the world, that he would accomplish all that was necessary so that everything would be made new again in Christ. He had a "secret purpose or will" that was not revealed in other ages that there would be a "new man" (Ephesians 2:15) made from both Jews and Gentiles and that it would be "Christ in you, the hope of glory" (Colossians 1:27). It was his determination alone that brought this secret to pass because the mystery was never revealed until God made it known to the apostle Paul. It says in 1 Peter that the angels desired to look into it, but they never saw the time period that we live in now. They and other prophets in the Old Testament saw that there was a break between the sufferings and the glory, but did not know what it was. It was God's secret! And ultimately, EVERYTHING will be new again in Christ.

Ephesians 1:11-12 continues to show the reason we were marked out beforehand. We are to show God's magnificence, to be to the praise of his glory as we saw in the last lesson.

Ephesians 1:11-12 APNT
And we were chosen in him, even as he marked us out beforehand and he willed, he who performs everything according to the purpose of his will, that we, those who first trusted in Christ, should be for the esteem of his magnificence.

Being "chosen in him" has to do with our inheritance. God marked us out to be his inheritance, his portion. When? He marked us out beforehand, before the foundations of the world! He called us and gave us the gift of his Spirit as a down payment to show us that we would have the complete inheritance in the fullness of times. If you read the verses without the phrases in the commas, it is simply, "he willed that we should be for the esteem of his magnificence." What does that mean? He gave us the Spirit so that we could demonstrate to the world his magnificent glory. Every time we walk by the Spirit, heal someone, prophesy, or speak revelation from God, we are demonstrating God's glory! That is our life now until we can come into the full redemption of our bodies when Christ comes back. Again, we should be shouting "Glory, hallelujah!" But most of all, we should get busy walking by the Spirit and learning all that we have in Christ!

OUR INHERITANCE

We learned in Lesson 3 that our inheritance in Christ is not the same as in our culture today or even in the lands and times of the Bible. In our culture, an inheritance is usually divided equally between all the children. In Israel, the firstborn son inherited a double portion. But our inheritance is as a "joint-heir" (Romans 8:17). That means we share fully in exactly the same portion as Jesus Christ received as a son. That is amazing!

Let's do a small word study to get a broader idea of what it means to be joint-heirs with Christ. These verses are great to meditate on. You can write some of your own thoughts and comments after the verses (as we did with the first verse in Lesson 2).

Christ is the heir of all things:

Hebrews 1:2 APNT
And in these last days, he has spoken to us by his Son, whom he appointed heir of everything and by whom he made the ages,

_____
_____
_____

We are joint heirs with Christ:

LESSON 5 ⯎ WHAT GOD DID BEFOREHAND

Romans 8:17 APNT
And if [we are] sons, [then] also heirs, heirs of God and fellow-heirs of Jesus Christ, that if we suffer with him, we will also be glorified with him.

_____
_____
_____

We are heirs of:

1. The promise to Abraham

Galatians 3:29 APNT
And if you are of Christ, then you are the seed of Abraham and heirs in the promise.

_____
_____
_____

Hebrews 6:17 APNT
Because of this, God especially wanted to show to the heirs of the promise that his promise would not change, so he bound it with oaths,

_____
_____
_____

2. Righteousness by faith

Hebrews 11:7 ESV
By faith Noah, being warned by God concerning events as yet unseen, in reverent fear constructed an ark for the saving of his household. By this he condemned the world and became an heir of the righteousness that comes by faith.

_____
_____
_____

3. The world

Romans 4:13 ESV
For the promise to Abraham and his offspring that he would be heir of the world did not come through the law but through the righteousness of faith.

_____
_____
_____

4. Salvation

Hebrews 1:14 ESV
Are they not all ministering spirits sent out to serve for the sake of those who are to inherit salvation?

_____
_____
_____

5. Eternal life

Titus 3:7 APNT
that we would be justified by his grace and would be heirs in the hope of eternal life.

_____
_____
_____

6. The kingdom

James 2:5 APNT
Hear, my beloved brothers, was it not the poor of the world, but [who are] rich in faith [that] God chose to be heirs in the kingdom that God promised to those who love him?

_____
_____
_____

7. Jews and Gentiles are fellow-heirs

Ephesians 3:6 ESV
This mystery is that the Gentiles are fellow heirs, members of the same body, and partakers of the promise in Christ Jesus through the gospel.

_____
_____
_____

So now we have a choice. We learned about everything that God did beforehand—he chose us beforehand to be his sons, holy and without blemish. He marked us out and engraved us on his hands beforehand. He determined beforehand to accomplish all that was necessary so that we might have the revelation of the mystery and have all the power of the risen Christ. And he marked us out beforehand for his inheritance so that we would be to the praise of his glory. All these things were done beforehand, before the foundations of the world. Are we going to walk in those works that he prepared for us or not? Are we willing to have our lives be to the praise of his glory?

FURTHER STUDY AND DISCUSSION

1. What kind of value does God place on you in light of calling you from before the foundation of the world?

2. What can you do right now to claim your inheritance?

3. Study the words "portion" and "lot." What do these words have to do with inheritance?
    Deuteronomy 32:9 KJV
    For the LORD'S portion is his people; Jacob is the lot of his inheritance.

LESSON 6 ✦ EXCEEDING GREATNESS OF HIS POWER

Have you ever experienced a power failure? There was one in San Diego a number of years ago and I was caught in the airport at the time. Thankfully my suitcase had already come down the carousel before the electricity shut off! But in those situations, there are many hardships and people are surprised by the lack of things we take for granted: lights, refrigerators, air conditioning, to name only a few.

The last section of the prayer in Ephesians 1:19 is that we would experience the exceeding greatness of God's power. This spiritual power never goes out!

KEY VERSE

Ephesians 1:19 APNT
and what is the abundance of the greatness of his power in us, in those who believe, according to the working of the might of his power.

If men ever needed anything, they need the power of God in their lives. The good news is that God offers his power to men and also guarantees the "working" of that power. It is available to experience fully. Let's take a look at what kind of power this is.

There are two uses of the figure of speech called *antimeria* in this verse. When there is a figure of speech, that is the part of the verse that is emphasized. In this verse, what is emphasized is "the abundance of the greatness of his power" and "the working of the might of his power." If you ever want to find out if there are figures of speech in a verse, go to Bullinger's *Figures of Speech in the Bible* and look up the verse in the index. In *antimeria,* the genitive case is used instead of an adjective to emphasize the last noun. In this verse, twice this figure is used with two nouns, so we could translate the phrases as "the great abundant power" and "the mighty energizing power." The Greek words for "great abundance" are *hupoballo megathos. Hupoballo* means exceeding, surpassing, unlimited, immeasurable. *Megathos* is mighty or explosive. We get the English word megaton which measures atomic explosives. Another way you could translate this phrase is "immeasurable explosive power." This is God's power, the power of God himself. He is the one who energizes it mightily.

We are sons of God with power! I have shared in my teachings that at one time I had a vision showing me what this kind of power was like. Before me was a huge steel door from the ceiling to the floor; the door was massive—at least ten feet thick. Then there appeared a gigantic bit, like the long spiral type used in a high-powered drill. The bit was all set up to go through the huge, thick wall. The only thing required of me was to turn the drill on to activate the bit. It easily penetrated the wall, not because of my strength but because of the strength of the drill. It didn't matter that the wall was thick. It didn't matter that it was made out of steel. What mattered was that the power of the drill was greater than the size and strength of the steel wall it was going through. That's the kind of power we are talking about here—the greatness of his power. It operates, it moves, it goes through seemingly impervious objects and as a result, something amazing happens! The power is not static, but dynamic and forceful.

The thing to note is that God's power is given to us to use. God's power is demonstrated in what he did for Christ. But now, as we believe, that power is released. Let's zero in on what kind of power this is.

1. Power that raised Christ from the dead

Ephesians 1:20 NET
This power he exercised in Christ when he raised him from the dead and seated him at his right hand in the heavenly realms

God's power raised Jesus Christ from the dead. He conquered death, which was the Evil One's greatest tool. The resurrection of Jesus Christ shows that God has the power to give man a new life and then also to give him the power to live that new life before him, now and in the future. We will also be raised from the dead! But in the meantime, we have that same power to use on a daily basis.

2. Power of the exalted Christ

When God raised Jesus from the dead, he exalted him to be seated at his right hand. That means that he has the highest seat of honor and authority in the universe.

Ephesians 1:21-22a APNT
higher than all rulers and authorities and powers and lordships and higher than every name that is named, not only in this world, but in the coming [one] also.
And he subjected everything under his feet ...

Christ is over every authority that could be named, including all of the Enemy's hosts.

Philippians 2:9-10 KJV
Wherefore God also hath highly exalted him, and given him a name which is above every name:

That at the name of Jesus every knee should bow, of things in heaven, and things in earth, and things under the earth;

The phrase "under his feet" has the figure of speech, *synecdoche,* where "feet" represents the victory over something. In the Old Testament battles, the winner would symbolically put his feet on the necks of the enemies in testimony of the victory (Joshua 10:24). This verse is also an allusion to Psalm 8:6 where man was given dominion over all the works of God's hands.

3. Power as the head of the Church—all in all

Ephesians 1:22b-23 APNT
and he gave him who is higher than all [to be] the head of the church,
which is his body and the fullness of him who is filling all in all.

Believers are to experience the power of God, the same power that made Jesus Christ the head of the Church. He has the supreme authority over the Church. The Church is his body and cannot function without the "head" or leader of it. Just as a head must have a body to carry out various functions, the body must have a head to direct and lead it.

If God had the power to create the Church and to make Christ the head, then he has the power to make the body function and work for Christ. This is the active "working of his mighty power." The working means "energizing."

God's power is great, abundant and explosive—the same power that raised Christ from the dead. It is supreme in function and authority and it is worked out and demonstrated in the Church. But now let's stop for a moment and zero in on a phrase in verse 23: "the fullness of him who is filling all in all." Sometimes we just read over phrases like this.

"All in all" has another figure of speech called *ellipsis.* "All" is an adjective and must have a noun or pronoun to which it refers. Since this is missing it needs to be supplied from the context. In Ephesians 1:23, we could supply the nouns as: "is filling all (spiritual gifts and grace) in all (the members of the body.)" In fact, there are a number of ways the ellipsis could be stated. Here are a few:

All things in all members
All grace in all situations
All power in all believers
All of you with all of him

EXERCISE

Look up the verse in multiple translations and you will see how many different ways this is translated. Here are a few suggestions:

VERSION	TRANSLATION
Amplified	
Weymouth	
CEV	
NLT	

To understand a little more about the word for "fullness" in Greek, look up the definition in *Thayer's Greek Lexicon* (go online to www.biblehub.com):

_____

_____

The following are other verses that have the phrase "all in all." Fill in what you think the ellipsis should be.

1 Corinthians 12:6   all_____ in all _____
1 Corinthians 15:28   all_____ in all _____
Colossians 3:11   all_____ in all _____

FURTHER STUDY AND DISCUSSION

1) How does knowing about this power help to understand Ephesians 6:10?

2) What is the connection between knowing God and the power of God?

3) Is there an area of your life that lacks God's power? How could it be filled?

LESSON 7 ⁂ THE GREAT MYSTERY UNRAVELED

A key theme in the book of Ephesians is "the great mystery." It is a theme that is crucial to understand so that other themes in the book are clear.

The idea of a mystery is that it is a hidden or secret thing, not obvious to the understanding. The definition of the Greek word for mystery, *musterion,* from *Thayer's Greek Lexicon* is: "the secret counsels which govern God in dealing with the righteous, which are hidden from ungodly and wicked men but plain to the godly." A further definition is: "in rabbinic writings, it denotes the mystic or hidden sense: a. of an OT saying, b. of an image or form seen in a vision, and c. of a dream."

From the time of the early Church Fathers, the word *musterion* took on the idea that it was something which could not be understood. This has carried through to our day and time, when we use the word mystery. It has the connotation that it cannot be known. But that is not true. As in the definition from Thayer above, it is usually hidden from ungodly men, but "plain to the godly." The rabbinic writings were accurate when they described a mystery as the hidden sense of something. It could be revealed by a vision, dream, or any method, but it is always a revealing from God. A summary definition could be "a spiritual secret."

Daniel 2:22 KJV
He revealeth the deep and secret things: he knoweth what is in the darkness, and the light dwelleth with him.

When Daniel received the revelation of the "secret" of Nebuchadnezzar's dream, he used the same Aramaic word for mystery in the New Testament, *raza.* The hidden things are revealed by God in his timing. Once they are revealed, they "belong to us and to our children forever."

Deuteronomy 29:29 NIV
The secret things belong to the LORD our God, but the things revealed belong to us and to our children forever, that we may follow all the words of this law.

Let's do a brief word study on the word for mystery. The verses are the same in both Greek and Aramaic.

1 Corinthians 2:7-10 APNT
but we speak the wisdom of God in a mystery, which was hidden and [which] God
determined beforehand, from before the ages, for our glory.
Not one of the authorities of this world knew, for if they had known it, they would not
have crucified the Lord of glory.
But as it is written: the eye has not seen and the ear has not heard and into the heart of
man has not entered what God has prepared for those who love him.
But God has revealed [it] to us by his Spirit, for the Spirit searches everything, even the
deep [things] of God.

These verses in 1 Corinthians refer to wisdom of God in a mystery that was hidden. God knows many "hidden" things and he reveals them by his Spirit to those who seek for the deep things. In this lesson, we are going to ask questions that make us think deeper about a topic. What do you think is an important point in this passage about the mystery?

_____
_____
_____

Romans 16:24-25 APNT
Now to God, who is able to establish you in my gospel that is proclaimed about Jesus
Christ by the revelation of the mystery that was hidden from the times of the ages,
but is revealed in this time by way of the writings of the prophets, and by the
commandment of the eternal God is made known to all the Gentiles for the obedience of
the faith,

What is the purpose of revealing the mystery? Who revealed it?

_____
_____
_____

1 Timothy 3:16 APNT
and truly great is this mystery of uprightness, which was revealed in the flesh and was
justified spiritually and was seen by angels and was preached among the Gentiles and
was believed in the world and was taken up in glory.

Prior to the revealing of the mystery, all of the blessings of God were given to the descendants of Abraham through Isaac and Jacob, who are called the Judeans or Jews.

If Gentiles wanted to be a part of the covenant God made with the Judeans, then they needed to become proselytes and convert to Judaism.

What other things does this verse tell us about the mystery? Who is the mystery about?

_____

_____

_____

Colossians 1:27 APNT
To them, God wanted to make known what is the wealth of the glory of this mystery among the Gentiles, which is the Messiah who is in you, the hope of our glory,

What kind of connotation does "riches" or "wealth" bring up in your mind?

_____

_____

_____

Now we will look in more detail at a summary verse about the mystery in Ephesians 3.

THREE ILLUSTRATIONS OF THE MYSTERY

Ephesians 3:6 KJV
That the Gentiles should be fellowheirs, and of the same body, and partakers of his promise in Christ by the gospel.

There are three illustrations of the mystery that are used in Ephesians: the household, the body and the temple. Each of the phrases in verse 6 shows one of these.

In order to get an understanding of this verse, first of all, we need to note two figures of speech in the Greek. One is *polysyndeton*, the multiple use of "ands," which sets apart and emphasizes each of the three phrases. Each phrase needs to have the most deliberate attention. The other figure of speech is *homeopropheron* or alliteration, which is "the repetition of the same letter or syllable at the commencement of successive words." The words "fellowheirs," "of the same body" and "partakers" each begin with the Greek word *sun* or variations of *sun*: *sunkleronomos*, *sussomos* and *summetochos*, respectively. *Sun* means "with, in conjunction with, united with, together in, something common to both, implying fellowship, union or agreement with." What is emphasized by the alliteration is "together with, united with."

Now let us look at the three distinct phrases. Each phrase is a summary of an illustration that is developed throughout Ephesians as well as in the other epistles.

The Gentiles are fellow-heirs or "together-heirs" with whom?

The only other place this word for fellow-heirs is used is in Romans 8:17 and it is translated "joint-heirs." Both Jews and Gentiles who are born again are joint-heirs with Christ. The mystery revealed is that both Jews and Gentiles would share fully in the inheritance with Christ. This first phrase emphasizes that the mystery is a family or household with God as the Father and with every member having all the rights and privileges of sons and a full inheritance.

The Gentiles are "of the same body" as whom?

The mystery revealed is that both Jews and Gentiles are inseparably linked with Christ as a unified whole, functioning together with him as the head. We are of the same body with Christ. It is Christ's body. This is the second illustration used of the mystery—that we are a body. It portrays how we practically live in our relationship with each other and with God and with Christ.

The Gentiles are "partakers" with whom?

The mystery revealed is that both Jews and Gentiles have a full sharing in all that Christ accomplished and the salvation he made available. We share fully in the promise to Abraham that the seed would come who would be the Messiah.

In Ephesians 3:6 the word "partakers" is *summetochos* and according to Moulton-Milligan, this Greek word was used in the business documents called papyri in the sense of a joint ownership, "joint possessors of a house." The holding we have in joint ownership is the gift of the Spirit and by that we are partakers of Christ.

But what is the "house" of which we are "joint-possessors"? This is explained in Ephesians that we are the temple of God and his habitation or dwelling place.

Ephesians 2:20b-22 ESV
...Christ Jesus himself being the cornerstone,
in whom the whole structure, being joined together, grows into a holy temple in the Lord.
In him you also are being built together into a dwelling place for God by the Spirit.

Hebrews 3:14 KJV
For we are made partakers of Christ…

We are partakers of God's habitation in Christ by the Spirit. This dwelling place of God is where we are seated (Ephesians 2:6). All the power and rest which was made available in Christ is ours together with him by way of the Spirit. The intimate fellowship and worship of God is ours also.

STRUCTURE OF EPHESIANS 3:4-7

Ephesians 3:4-7 ESV
When you read this, you can perceive my insight into the mystery of Christ,
which was not made known to the sons of men in other generations as it has now been revealed to his holy apostles and prophets by the Spirit.
This mystery is that the Gentiles are fellow heirs, members of the same body, and partakers of the promise in Christ Jesus through the gospel.
Of this gospel I was made a minister according to the gift of God's grace, which was given me by the working of his power.

All three of these phrases emphasize being united with, or in conjunction with Christ, "in HIM." It was in Christ that the mystery was unfolded. We who formerly were Jews or Gentiles are now joint-heirs with Christ! We are of Christ's body! We share fully in all that Christ accomplished!

This unique fellowship can be seen even more vividly by a study of the structure of Ephesians 3:6.

The last phrase "by the Spirit" of Ephesians 3:5 parallels "in Christ" in verse 6. Charles Welch in his book, *The Testimony of the Lord's Prisoner,* describes the structure in the following way as an alternation that is like a "sandwich":

A) now revealed to holy apostles and prophets
   B) by (in) the Spirit
   C) fellow heirs
   C) of the same body
   C) partakers of his promise
   B) in Christ
A) by the gospel

He then elaborates that the mystery is:

> bounded by the terms 'in Spirit' and 'in Christ' and has a three-fold equality, a fellowship without precedent.... The words 'in Spirit' of verse 5 do not refer to the revelation made to the apostles and prophets, but, as at the end of Ephesians ii, indicate the only sphere in which such an equality is possible.[2]

It is by or in the Spirit that we are "together with" Christ. The gift of the Holy Spirit is the "something common" which links us inseparably together in Christ.

1 Corinthians 12:13 KJV
For by one Spirit are we all baptized into one body, whether we be Jews or Gentiles, whether we be bond or free; and have been all made to drink into one Spirit.

We are "of the same body" with Christ for we are all baptized by one Spirit. This is the unique tie that binds the body of Christ together—we each have the exact same gift of Holy Spirit! That is what makes us one.

Ephesians 3:6 is the great mystery revealed in a nutshell. It is a summary of three major points which we have by the Spirit and in Christ. "By the Spirit" is the something common which unites both Gentile and Judean. "In Christ" is with whom we are united and how and why we have this union. We are fellow-heirs in Christ and are part of the great family and household of God, entitled to a full inheritance. We are one body in Christ and are thus a unified functioning whole. We are partakers together in Christ, sharing fully in all that he accomplished and all that he has and will have. We are of the household of God, of the body of Christ and are the temple of God. This is the mystery which WAS secret, but is "now revealed" and unraveled!

To cement the idea of these three illustrations of the mystery, you can spend some time looking up references in the book of Ephesians, but also the other epistles that are about each one. Use the key words below:

FAMILY OR HOUSEHOLD

_____
_____
_____

---

[2] Welch, Charles, *The Testimony of the Lord's Prisoner*, p. 82-88.

BODY

_____
_____
_____

TEMPLE OR BUILDING

_____
_____
_____

FURTHER STUDY AND DISCUSSION

1. Imagine yourself in a writing contest. Your assignment is to share in one sentence each what your membership in the family, the body and the temple means to you.

2. Which illustration do you relate to the most?

3. What is the gospel of the mystery? Can you answer that question in a few words?

LESSON 8 ⸕ JESUS CHRIST, THE COMPLETE FOUNDATION

One time, my husband Glen and I were visiting Zion National Park and I wanted to bring home some of the lava rocks that we saw everywhere. Of course, we didn't do that but I had come home and found our fireplace was full of those same lava rocks. Now the difference between a lava rock and the same shape rock of a different kind such as granite is in the weight and density of the rock. That is the same difference between religion and true Christianity. Christ is the rock on which everything else rests as a complete foundation.

In the ancient world, rocks were abundant in all kinds of shapes and sizes and used for many things, including building houses and other types of buildings. So rocks and stones became a ready image or metaphor to use to describe other things to understand.

During Passover, Psalm 118 was read and perhaps sung. It is about the Messiah and how he would be a stone that builders would reject, but would become the cornerstone. During Jesus' triumphant entry into Jerusalem, the people were singing "Hosanna" (save us) and "Blessed is he who comes in the name of the Lord" from this passage.

Psalm 118:21-26 ESV
I thank you that you have answered me and have become my salvation.
The stone that the builders rejected has become the cornerstone.
This is the LORD's doing; it is marvelous in our eyes.
This is the day that the LORD has made; let us rejoice and be glad in it.
Save us, we pray, O LORD! O LORD, we pray, give us success!
Blessed is he who comes in the name of the LORD! We bless you from the house of the LORD.

There are three main views of Christ as the Rock. They each contribute a slightly different view to be able to comprehend how Christ is the complete foundation.

1) Foundation stone
2) Cornerstone, head of the corner
3) Tried stone

Isaiah 28:16 lists all three different views of the stone to help us understand how Jesus Christ is the complete foundation.

Isaiah 28:16 NASB
Therefore thus says the Lord God, "Behold, I am laying in Zion a stone, a tested stone, A costly cornerstone for the foundation, firmly placed. He who believes in it will not be disturbed."

The Targum of this verse says: "he shall not be moved when trouble comes." He who believes on this foundation will not be ashamed (as it is quoted in 1 Peter 2:6). I want this, don't you? Let's take a look at the three views.

FOUNDATION STONE

Isaiah describes the foundation as "firmly placed." A foundation is what a building depends on for its structural integrity. God asked Job when he confronted him about who had laid the foundation of the earth.

Job 38:4-6 ESV
Where were you when I laid the foundation of the earth? Tell me, if you have understanding.
Who determined its measurements—surely you know! Or who stretched the line upon it?
On what were its bases sunk, or who laid its cornerstone,

The earth has a foundation on which its bases were sunk. These are like the footings that builders today still lay in order to pour a foundation. The measurements are determined and the foundation is laid out via a plumb line so it is evenly spaced.

Look up Acts 4:10-12 in your favorite version. This is another place where Isaiah 28:16 is quoted in the New Testament. How does it show that Jesus is the foundation stone?

_____
_____
_____

Can you think of another example of a foundation with which you are familiar?

_____
_____
_____

CORNERSTONE

The cornerstone or head of the corner was the most important stone in the building. It set the level, angle and outer dimensions of the building. It had to be squared true (vertically) so that all the other stones could be set from it. It covered the corner so each wall could be built on its platform. As we have seen in other lessons, everything in the New Testament Church is to be built on Christ.

Ephesians 2:18-22 ESV
For through him we both have access in one Spirit to the Father.
So then you are no longer strangers and aliens, but you are fellow citizens with the saints and members of the household of God,
built on the foundation of the apostles and prophets, Christ Jesus himself being the cornerstone,
in whom the whole structure, being joined together, grows into a holy temple in the Lord.
In him you also are being built together into a dwelling place for God by the Spirit.

In Christ, the whole temple is being built as a dwelling place for God. The dimensions are set by lining up with the measurements of Christ: his peace, his love, his mind, his wisdom, the full measure of the Spirit. The structure is "fitly framed together" (King James Version) where each stone (son) is perfectly placed. The word for son in Hebrew is *ben* and the word for stone is *eben*. This is a play on words about how God wanted sons to dwell in and he compares them to stones.

1 Peter has another quotation of Isaiah 28 where we can see how we are living stones that are measured on the cornerstone of Christ.

1 Peter 2:4-6 APNT
The one to whom you are drawn is the living stone that men have rejected, yet with God [is] chosen and honored.
And you also, as living stones, are built up and are spiritual temples and holy priests to offer spiritual sacrifices that are acceptable before God by way of Jesus Christ.
For it is told in the scripture: behold, I lay in Zion an approved and precious stone in the head of the corner and he who believes on him will not be ashamed.

From the context of this passage and from other verses we have read so far, list some things that we are doing in this living temple. What kind of spiritual sacrifices are in this temple?

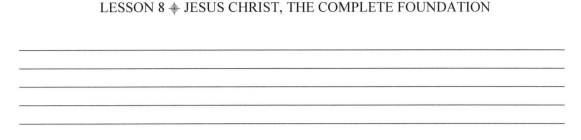

TRIED STONE

Continuing on in the section of 1 Peter, the same cornerstone is called "a stone of stumbling."

1 Peter 2:7-8 APNT
Therefore, this honor is given to you who believe. But to those who are not convinced, he is a stone of stumbling and a rock of offense. And they stumbled at him [it], in that they were not persuaded by the word to which they were appointed.

Verse 8 is a quotation of Isaiah 8:14. Here is one version of this verse. You could look up a few versions to get the variety of how offense and stumbling are translated.

Isaiah 8:14-15 KJV
And he shall be for a sanctuary; but for a stone of stumbling and for a rock of offence to both the houses of Israel, for a gin and for a snare to the inhabitants of Jerusalem.
And many among them shall stumble, and fall, and be broken, and be snared, and be taken.

A tried stone is one which is tested and found to be worthy to be the cornerstone. It is also a testing stone for other "stones" to see how they will fit into the temple. People who believe are not ashamed, but for those who don't believe, the cornerstone becomes a stone of stumbling. In our western world of concrete and asphalt, we don't have as many occasions for stumbling. But in the ancient Roman empire, roads were not paved, but made of rocks fitted together. When I was in Israel, it was amazing to me how uneven the paths were when paved with rocks.

There are two things that happen to someone who rejects Christ as the cornerstone and foundation. Either they fall on the stone (stumble) or the stone falls on them (offense). The chief priests and Pharisees were prominent in rejecting Jesus Christ, but this applies to anyone who rejects Christ.

Matthew 21:42-25 APNT
Jesus said to them, "Have you never read in the scripture of the stone that the builders rejected? It has become the head of the corner. This [stone] came from the presence of the Lord and it is a wonder in our eyes.
Because of this, I say to you, the kingdom of God will be taken away from you and be given to a people who bear fruit.
And whoever falls on this stone will be bruised, and whomever it falls on, it will blow him away [as chaff]."
And when the chief priests and Pharisees heard his parables, they knew that he spoke against them.

Read Daniel 2:34-45 which is the explanation of the vision of Nebuchadnezzar about the end times. Note particularly verses 34-35 and 44-45 to see how Jesus Christ as the stone is going to smash all the other kingdoms of the world and set up a kingdom that will stand forever. You can write some notes here of your observations.

_____
_____
_____
_____
_____
_____

FURTHER STUDY AND DISCUSSION

1. Is Christ your sanctuary or stone of stumbling? In what areas could there be improvement?

2. What do you think of this quote from the entry on "stumbling block" in *Dictionary of Biblical Imagery*?
    "A little misstep of the feet, a sudden trip over an unseen obstacle, the awkward and suspended moment of uncertain recovery or fall, these are the common experiences of life on two legs."

3. Sometimes cornerstone is described as a capstone or keystone. This comes from the architecture of Roman times and later. It is sometimes used to compare Christ as the "First and the Last." Do you agree with this analogy and that it should be part of this study?

LESSON 9 ⚜ THE DWELLING PLACE OF GOD

In the last lesson we learned that one of the illustrations of the mystery is the temple and that this temple is the dwelling place of God. But why is this such an important illustration?

<u>KEY VERSE</u>

Ephesians 2:20b-22 ESV
...Christ Jesus himself being the cornerstone,
in whom the whole structure, being joined together, grows into a holy temple in the Lord.
In him you also are being built together into a dwelling place for God by the Spirit.

Let's take a closer look at this passage on the doctrinal side of Ephesians. The illustration of the temple shows who we are as the Church in Christ. In order to understand the two verses above, a key to interpretation of scripture is that we look at the context. The whole of chapter 2 weaves a portrait of what the temple of God is and how it is built.

Ephesians 2:4-7 APNT
But God, who is rich in his mercies, because of his great love [with] which he loved us, while we were dead in our sins, gave us life with Christ and, by his grace, redeemed us and raised us with him and seated us with him in heaven in Jesus Christ,
so that he could show to the ages that are coming the greatness of the wealth of his grace and his goodness that is to us in Jesus Christ.

Even while we were dead, God saved us (gave us life), redeemed us, raised us with Christ and seated us with him in the heavenlies. These four things are the mark of every individual in the Church. God has redeemed us from death to life and given us all the authority of Christ.

Ephesians 2:8-10 APNT
For by his grace we were redeemed by faith and this was not from yourselves, but is the gift of God,
not from works, so that no one would boast.
For we [are] his own creation, who are created in Jesus Christ for good works, those [works] which God prepared previously that we should walk in.

Then we learn that this redemption is by grace and is a gift from God. We also learn that we are "his own creation" not *by* works, but that we are given good works to do. This will be important to remember when we see how the temple is supposed to function. The word translated "creation" in the Aramaic is *beritha* and the companion Hebrew word in the Old Testament is *bara*. It is first used in Genesis 1 when God created the heavens and the earth and also "man in his own image." (Genesis 1:27) God's image was Spirit and when God calls us his "workmanship" it means that is the restoration of the time of Adam when God put Spirit in man.

Ephesians 2:12-15 APNT
And at that time, you were without Christ and you were aliens from the customs of Israel and you were strangers to the covenant of the promise and you were without hope and without God in the world.
But now, in Jesus Christ, you who previously were far have become near by the blood of Christ.
For he was our peace treaty, who made the two of them one and has broken down the wall that stood in the middle
and the conflict, by his flesh. And he brought to an end the law of commandments with its commandments, so that [from] the two of them he would create in himself one new man, and he made a peace treaty.

The next part of chapter 2 describes how the Gentiles were cut off from the fellowship of the tabernacle and the temple worship and were "without God." They did not have a way to come into God's presence. The "middle wall of partition" was in the temple in the first century where there was a wall separating the outer court from the inner court. There were inscribed stones along the edge of this court which said: "No one, being a foreigner, may enter into the enclosure around the holy place. Whosoever is apprehended will himself be to blame for his death which will certainly follow."[3] All Gentiles were "foreigners." Now God made peace between the Jews and Gentiles by creating a totally new entity based on Christ and so destroyed the conflict.

Ephesians 2:16-18 APNT
And he reconciled the two of them with God in one body and, by his cross, he destroyed the conflict.
And he came [and] HE DECLARED PEACE TO YOU, [BOTH] THE FAR AND THE NEAR,
because in him we both have access in one spirit to the Father.

---

[3] Welch. Charles. *In Heavenly Places*, p. 234.

There were more separations in the temple besides the middle wall. There was a section where only Jews could enter. Then another where only Jewish men could enter. Then another where only the priests could serve and finally the Holy of Holies where only once a year the high priest could enter. All of these "walls" were torn down and the way into the inner sanctuary was made open. Both Jews and Gentiles now have access to this inner sanctuary because of having been given one Spirit.

Ephesians 2:19-20 APNT
From now on, you are neither strangers nor foreigners, but citizens who are holy [ones] and [of] the household of God.
And you are built on the foundation of the apostles and of the prophets and Jesus Christ is the head of the corner of the building.

Now we are instructed that we are not only not strangers anymore (as in verse 12), but we are not foreigners either. This begins the introduction to a number of words related to the word for "to build" and "house." These are the word families of a particular verb. Below is a chart with the Greek words in the family of *domeo* (build) and *oikos* (house).

VERSE	ENGLISH WORD	GREEK WORD	MEANING
19	Foreigner	*Paroikos*	One who lives in a place with no rights of citizenship
19	Household	*Oikeios*	Belonging to a family or house
20	Built	*Epoikodomeo*	Build a house on
21	Building	*Oikodome*	A house built
22	Built together	*Sunoikodomeo*	Build a house together as a whole
22	Dwelling place	*Katoiketerion*	Dwelling

As we saw in the last lesson, in Aramaic and Hebrew, there is a close relation between the words for son and stone. Another related word is "to build." Son is *ben*, stone is *eben* and build is *banah*. A son is someone who continues the life of the family and a building comes from this continuing of life. The relation to stone is then seen as the permanent continuing of life because a stone building in the eastern culture was the strongest form of construction. Sons make up the building (temple) of God and they are like stones.

Now we can look at Ephesians 2:21-22 more closely.

Ephesians 2:21 APNT
And in him the whole building is fit together and is growing into a holy temple in the LORD,

"Fit together" means to be organized compactly, joined and united and connected to Christ as the foundation. The gift of the Spirit is the cement that bonds the building together. This building is "growing," meaning it is continually being added to. The Greek of "the whole building" means every part of the building. It could be likened to a building complex but all built on one foundation.

The purpose of building a house is so that someone may live in it. This building is a holy (consecrated) place where God dwells. Even in the Old Testament, the temple was called "the house of the Lord" or the "house of God" (see Psalm 23:6). The Church of Jesus Christ does not worship at a temple but has *become* the temple. God now lives both among and with (in) his people—not in a literal building, but in a living community.

Ephesians 2:22 ESV
In him you also are being built together into a dwelling place for God by the Spirit.

EXERCISE

Let's pause here and summarize what we have learned. An easy way to do this is to write out other verses where it calls the Church the building or the temple. Note that "you" or "your" is always plural in these verses.

1 Corinthians 3:9

_____

_____

_____

LESSON 9 ⊹ THE DWELLING PLACE OF GOD

1 Corinthians 3:16-17

_____
_____
_____

1 Corinthians 6:19

_____
_____
_____

2 Corinthians 6:16

_____
_____
_____

In the last verse above, find the passage(s) in the Old Testament where this is quoted from.

_____
_____
_____

Lastly, I would like for us to ponder what goes on in a temple or the dwelling place of God. We learned earlier that there are good works to walk in. 1 Peter calls us "living stones."

1 Peter 2:5 ESV
you yourselves like living stones are being built up as a spiritual house, to be a holy priesthood, to offer spiritual sacrifices acceptable to God through Jesus Christ.

What would parallels be to the Old Testament sacrifices? (see context of 1 Peter 2:9)

_____
_____

The word "built up" in verse 5 is *oikodomeo* and as we learned it means to "build the house." It is also translated "edify" and the noun is "edification." This is the primary thing that is to be done in the Church. Edify means to promote growth, bless, teach, encourage, love.

Look up the uses of "edifying" and "edification" in the New Testament and make a list of things that can be done (the good works) in the temple (dwelling place of God).

_____
_____
_____
_____
_____
_____
_____

FURTHER STUDY AND DISCUSSION

1. How does the Church grow? Name some ways.

2. What did Jesus Christ mean in Matthew 16:18?

3. How does the temple compare to a person who has body, soul and spirit?

LESSON 10 ♦ THE BALANCED WALK

The Word of God sets forth very clearly what our walk should be like and how to walk. The word "walk" is a Hebrew idiom, meaning to live. To walk means "to regulate one's life, to conduct oneself." When the Bible shows what our walk should be like, it shows how we should regulate our lives and conduct ourselves.

The use of the term "to walk" to describe living and conducting ourselves is singularly apropos. If we look for a moment at what a physical, literal walk is not, it will be easy to see this. A walk is not a run. It is slower, steadier, where there is plenty of time to look around at the scenery. Compared to running, a walk does not require extreme exertion of energy. A walk is not a sprint. Sprinting means running full force but only for a limited time and distance. A man could walk steadily at a reasonable pace for almost as long as necessary (especially with daily periods of sleep!) To walk is not to be a gymnast or a wrestler or involved in any other particular sport which would require very highly developed muscles and skills. Not everyone is able to be a great gymnast, but everyone can be a great walker. Several other contrasts to note are: to walk does not mean to take a few steps and sit down. It implies continuous movement. Also, a walk is a relatively small step by small step process, not the broad jump or flying leaps of dancers. It can be slow or fast-paced, but it is always one step at a time, one foot following the other. That is why it is such a great idiom to compare walking to how we live our lives.

With these things in mind, the first verse on the practical side of Ephesians talks about how we should live. The first way our walk is described is by using an adjective, *axios*, meaning "worthily or in balance."

KEY VERSE

Ephesians 4:1 ESV
I therefore, a prisoner for the Lord, urge you to walk in a manner worthy of the calling to which you have been called,

Walking worthily or "in a manner worthy" is to walk in balance. If we relate this to physical walking, we can understand how crucial it is. If we walked with our bodies tipped far to the right or left, or even backward or forward, it would be very difficult to get anywhere. God designed the physical body to walk in an upright position, in balance. Our life walk is to be held in balance, "of the calling," having both doctrinal and practical sides. This verse introduces the last half of Ephesians which is all about the practical walk.

The results of this balanced walk of life are stated further in Colossians. To walk physically, even as doctors and health advisors say, is the best exercise where almost all areas of the body are strengthened and vitalized.

Colossians 1:10-11 KJV
That ye might walk worthy of the Lord unto all pleasing, being fruitful in every good work, and increasing in the knowledge of God;
Strengthened with all might, according to his glorious power, unto all patience and longsuffering with joyfulness;

The results of a balanced walk in the Lord, in fellowship with him are: 1) fruitfulness in *every* good work, 2) increasing, abounding in the knowledge of God, 3) being strengthened with all might, and 4) patience and longsuffering with joyfulness.

There are three main Greek prepositions that are used to describe walking: *en*—being or remaining in with the primary idea of rest or continuance, *dia*—by, through, by way of, as being a standard, and *kata*—according to, "the horizontal motion along which the action proceeds." These three prepositions are used with the word "walk" very distinctly in Greek. But in Aramaic, there is only one preposition which could be translated in various ways as "in, by, according to, by way of and with." When this is the case, it is interesting to substitute a broader preposition instead of narrowing the interpretation down to only the meaning of the Greek.

For example, Ephesians 5:2 says to "walk in love." This is the Greek preposition *en.* Then it means to dwell in love and rest in it. But if we substitute "according to," then it means the outward horizontal relationships of love and how they are acted out. If we substitute "by," then there is emphasis on a standard by which we live which is love.

EXERCISE

On the next page is a chart of the uses of *peripateo* (walk) + *en* (in). Read and study the verses and fill in comments on the chart of what the verse and its immediate context say about how to walk like this (or not) and the results of walking in something specific.

VERSE	POSITIVE	NEGATIVE	HOW	RESULTS
John 8:12		In darkness		
John 11:9	In the day			
John 11:10		In the night		
John 12:25		In the darkness		
Romans 6:4	In newness of life			
2 Cor 4:2		In craftiness		
2 Cor 10:3	In the flesh	After (*kata*) the flesh		
Eph 2:10	In good works			
Eph 4:17		In vanity of mind		
Eph 5:2	In love			
Col 2:6	In him			
Col 4:5	In wisdom			
Heb 13:9		Diverse and strange doctrines		
1 John 1:6		In darkness		
1 John 1:7	In light			
1 John 2:11		In darkness		
2 John 4	In truth			
2 John 6	In his commandments			
3 John 3	In truth			
3 John 4	In truth			

These are not the only verses about walking, but as you can see there starts to be a pattern of repetition of certain contrasts such as light and darkness, flesh and spirit, truth versus craftiness, wisdom and vanity of our own minds, to name only a few. You could also make another chart with these contrasts. Now take a look at all of the prepositions "in" and substitute "by" or "according to."

WALK—HOW?

There are also several adverbs which tell us HOW to walk and not walk. We already saw the word "worthily." The next adverb used with walk is *euschemos*, meaning honestly, becomingly. Physically I think of walking gracefully, head held high, shoulders back. In life it means to conduct one's life with integrity and with grace. Integrity and honesty in all of our dealings in life is crucial to have good results. Gracefulness and ease come in life by living in and by God's grace. He made us lovely and acceptable in his sight (Ephesians 1:4). These two factors, integrity and grace, make our walk, our life, beautiful.

1 Thessalonians 4:12 KJV
That ye may walk honestly toward them that are without, and that ye may have lack of nothing.

That is a great promise for this life: if we walk honestly, we will have lack of nothing. It reminds me of many other promises in the Bible, such as Matthew 6:33, Philippians 4:16 and 2 Corinthians 9:8.

The third adverb, *akribos*, is used with "walk" in only one verse in Ephesians 5:15 and in the King James Version is translated "circumspectly."

Ephesians 5:15-17 APNT
Therefore, see how you should walk accurately, not as fools, but as wise [ones]
who buy their opportunity, because the days are evil.
Because of this, do not be stupid, but understand what is the will of God.

Some of the definitions of *akribos* are diligently, precisely, with perfect manner, or accurately. It was used in Greek literature to describe how a person would climb a mountain. A related word, *akribestatos,* is used in Acts 26:5 where Paul described himself as living "after the most straightest sect of our religion" as a Pharisee. How to walk circumspectly is spelled out in the following verses in Ephesians 5. We need to redeem the time, take advantage of every opportunity to serve, to love and to care, by determining and understanding what the will of the Lord is. He will guide us in a precise manner even though we are in the middle of evil days.

The fourth word used with "walk" is the adverb, *ataktos*. This word means "irregularly, disorderly, unruly." It is used two times in 2 Thessalonians 3.

2 Thessalonians 3:6, 11-12 KJV
Now we command you, brethren, in the name of our Lord Jesus Christ, that ye withdraw yourselves from every brother that walketh disorderly, and not after the tradition which he received of us.
For we hear that there are some which walk among you disorderly, working not at all, but are busybodies.
Now them that are such we command and exhort by our Lord Jesus Christ, that with quietness they work, and eat their own bread.

The tradition that they received from Paul was not a certain method of work, but a lifestyle where he diligently and quietly worked to take care of his own physical needs. That is what "disorderly" is: to expect others to always take care of you and to be busybodies, meddling in other people's affairs. It says not to "hang out" with people who live like that. To say this positively, one should live his life with quietness, taking care of his own family. This reminds me of Titus 1:7-11 which is the passage that describes the qualifications of a bishop or elder. An elder should be *"a lover of hospitality, a lover of good men, sober, just, holy, temperate; holding fast the faithful word as he hath been taught…"*

The last adjective used with "walk" is the word for acting uprightly, *orthopodeo*. It literally means to be "straight-footed." It is to walk in a straight line, not crookedly. The passage where this word is used is in Galatians 2 when Peter came to Antioch and influenced other believers to go back to the Jewish customs.

Galatians 2:14 APNT
And when I saw that they were not walking correctly in the truth of the gospel, I said to Peter in front of all of them, "If you who are a Judean live as a heathen and not as a Judean, how can you compel the Gentiles to live as a Judean?"

Truth is the straight course by which we walk. If we veer off the path and walk according to the traditions of men, we will not be "straight-footed." I believe this straight path has to do with not getting tricked by all the fronts of idolatry. Idolatry—not putting God first—is disguised by self, others, the environment and religion. Anyone who looks at anything other than God and his Word will start to walk in that direction and end up stepping aside. That is what happened to Peter in Antioch and we can prevent it from happening to us when we walk on the straight path of truth.

These five descriptions of how to walk paint a beautifully complete picture of the kind of conduct we should have in our everyday life. We are to keep in balance, not emphasizing doctrine more than practice. We are to live with honesty and integrity and thus will have lack of nothing. We are to walk with accuracy and precision, discerning what the will of the Lord is. We are to live in quietness, working to take care of our own affairs. We are to walk straight-footed on the truth of the gospel and not be tricked by any traditions of men. The walk of the Word is like physical walking, keeping upright, head and shoulders back, one precise step at a time on a straight path.

FURTHER STUDY AND DISCUSSION

1) Read Ephesians 4:17-24 and note some of the ways the "Gentiles" walk and how a believer should be different than that.

2) How is a believer to walk after Christ? (See verses 20-24)

3) Can you understand and explain 2 Corinthians 5:7, "we walk by faith and not by sight," better after this study?

LESSON 11 ♦ KEEPING THE UNITY OF THE SPIRIT

Keeping the unity of the Spirit is a hot topic these days. It has almost become a "buzz word" in Christian circles. If you as an individual or a ministry are not promoting it, you are considered "out of sync" with the times. But, be that as it may, I wonder if a believer would have solid biblical answers for: What is unity? What is it based on? How does one promote it? These are the questions addressed in this lesson.

KEY VERSE

Ephesians 4:3 KJV
Endeavouring to keep the unity of the Spirit in the bond of peace.

What is unity? I love to study the Eastern languages, Hebrew and Aramaic, because abstract concepts (such as unity) are usually based on an action verb as the root of the word family. In other words, we can learn what the concept means by identifying the root verb and its action. The abstract concept is linked with this action and can be understood more thoroughly by looking at the root action. Unity comes from a verb root in Aramaic that means simply, "to turn towards a place or person with interest or affection." An intensive form of the verb means, "to cause to turn towards, or reconcile." An example of this verb usage is in Matthew.

Matthew 5:25 KJV
Agree with thine adversary quickly, whiles thou art in the way with him; lest at any time the adversary deliver thee to the judge and the judge deliver thee to the officer, and thou be cast into prison.

The Aramaic root verb, *aoa*, is the word "agree." Obviously, if the man in this verse agreed already, his opponent would not be called an adversary and they would not be on the way to the court. Agree here means "to settle or reconcile, to make an alliance." The way that is done can be seen in this verse. Stop on the road, sit down, turn towards one another, talk things out and cause an alliance to be made. (One note here—probably not all the differences are completely worked out, but enough to be a settling of the dispute.)

Keeping in mind that there is an action base in the word for unity, let us briefly examine this verse. "Be diligent" implies that this takes effort. "Keep" means to guard or watch over. We are to guard our lives so that this unity is maintained. What is the unity based on? Unity is "of the Spirit." When a believer turns to another believer with interest and affection, what should happen is an instant recognition that the other has THE SAME HOLY SPIRIT in them!

Ephesians 2:18 KJV
For through him we both have access by one Spirit unto the Father.

That same Spirit is the touchpoint, if you will, that stirs our interest and desire to form some kind of bond.

We learned in Lesson 9 regarding the temple that we have peace with each other because the walls have been broken down. Ephesians 2:17 says that *"he came and declared peace to you."* There is peace because of the one Spirit. The Aramaic word for "peace" in Ephesians 2:14-15 is not the usual word for peace, but it means peace treaty. Sound like the word for unity? I believe it has the same idea or implication as unity. Jesus Christ formed a peace treaty between the Jews and Gentiles because he gave the same gift of the Spirit to each one.

Peace in the New Testament is also used in the context of the body of Christ and living the mystery. The gospel or glad tidings of peace are that each believer has the gift of the Spirit born in them, but also that they have a special place in a body. They are members in particular. It brings peace to know that your particular place is unique in the body of Christ. There is no competition or vying for position, because the head, the Lord Jesus Christ, directs your unique function. Unity then is based on the fact that each believer has the same gift that is the measure of Christ AND each believer is a member in particular in the body of Christ.

But how do we promote unity? The word for "bond" in Ephesians 4:3 can be translated as girdle or band. The only other place in the New Testament where this word "girdle" is used is in Colossians 3:14 (APNT): *"And with all these [things], [put on] love, which is the girdle of maturity."* Maturity characterizes a person who puts on love as a girdle. Now we have a different picture in America for girdle than they did in the East, but I believe it is appropriate to think about for a moment here. A lady who is somewhat overweight will wear a girdle (or Spanx today) to "hold it all in" or to have a more slimming appearance. Isn't that what love does? It "holds it all in" and definitely makes for a more pleasing presentation! In the East, a girdle tied the robe around the waist so it would not come loose and fall off, and one could walk and carry on business without trying to continually hold the robe closed. Love is like that—it enables us to walk and carry on our own business. Love binds people together. Love is the mark of a mature Christian.

When we "turn to someone with interest or affection" and realize he is a believer, we have an instant recognition that he has the same gift of the Spirit and the same Lord we do. That gives us a touchpoint that helps us to hurdle any of the other differences. Then we rejoice because we can also recognize the "Christ in" the other person and how we each have a special place and function in the body of Christ. We can then promote that unity with love, tying relationships together and developing in maturity, promoting a peace treaty. This is keeping the unity of the Spirit in the bond of peace.

I want to make a comment here about something I have heard many times. If I turn to another, but they turn away from me and do not want to have anything to do with me, neither recognizing the Spirit or Christ in me or my function in the body of Christ, should I not turn away from them also and avoid any contact? First of all, Ephesians 4:3 is the last half of a sentence that begins, "walk worthy of the calling…." That means YOU walk worthy of the calling by being diligent to keep the unity of the Spirit. It is not talking about anybody else doing this but you. That means me, also. I have to obey the commandment of the Word of God and practice this. It does not depend on the response of others. Of course, relationships cannot be forced to happen unless two parties are willing to "turn to one another." However, I can, whenever another believer comes into my path, "turn towards him with affection" and still recognize that he has the same gift of the Spirit and a unique function in the body of Christ. I can do this, no matter what his response is.

In the last lesson we learned about walking in balance or worthy of our calling. There are four ways that are described how to walk worthily and how to be diligent to keep the unity of the Spirit. These are in the first three verses of Ephesians 4.

Ephesians 4:1-3 APNT
I, therefore, a prisoner in our Lord, beg you that you should walk as is proper for the calling that you were called,
with all humbleness of mind and quietness and long-suffering. And hold up one another in love
and be diligent to keep the alliance of the Spirit with the girdle of peace,

1. Humbleness of mind (meekness)
2. Quietness (gentleness)
3. Longsuffering (patience)
4. Holding up one another (forbearance)

EXERCISE

We are going to study these phrases from both Greek and Aramaic and summarize their meanings. But first, please take a regular dictionary and look up these words and write the main definition in English.

1. Meekness

   _____
   _____
   _____

2. Gentleness

   _____
   _____
   _____

3. Patience

   _____
   _____
   _____

4. Forbearance

   _____
   _____
   _____

Now we will first look at the Greek words. Use an online lexicon or Thayer's lexicon and look up the definitions of the Strong's numbers.

1. #5012 *tapheinophrosune*

   _____
   _____
   _____

2. #4236 *praotes*

   _____
   _____
   _____

3. #3115 *makrothumia*

_____
_____
_____

4. #430 *anechomai*

_____
_____
_____

Now we will look up the definitions of the Aramaic words. You can use the online database at www.aramaicdb.lightofword.org or the *Dictionary Number Lexicon* from LWM Publications. Enter the dictionary number in the Lexicon Search.

1. LWM #1356 *makikutha*

_____
_____
_____

2. LWM #1486 *nikhutha*

_____
_____
_____

3. LWM #1467 *nagirutha*

_____
_____
_____

4. LWM #1588 *sevar* (in Paiel tense – see notes)

_____
_____
_____

There are some variations in the meanings of the phrases between Greek and Aramaic, but we are not going to try to choose which one is better. Now we can actually put the definitions together with the English definitions to get the broadest understanding.

1. Meekness

    _____
    _____
    _____

2. Gentleness

    _____
    _____
    _____

3. Patience

    _____
    _____
    _____

4. Forbearance

    _____
    _____
    _____

There are no distinctly right answers in this exercise. The objective is to come up with as broad an understanding of these four phrases as possible. Now add this understanding to the lesson on keeping the unity of the Spirit. Without these qualities in a balanced walk, it will be extremely difficult to actually practice "turning to someone with interest and affection." But with these four characteristics figuring prominently in our lives, it is VERY possible to seek for and uphold the unity of the Spirit.

FURTHER STUDY AND DISCUSSION

1) What would be the opposite (negative side) of these four characteristics and how would that cause division instead of unity?

2) 1 Corinthians 1:10 says to be united in "one thought and one purpose." Reading the context of this verse, what insight can you gain in conjunction with Ephesians 4:3?

3) There are seven "ones" in Ephesians 4:4-6. What are they? How do they help to understand how to keep the unity of the Spirit?

LESSON 12 ✦ JESUS CHRIST, THE HEAD OF THE BODY

The illustration of the Church as a body is described in detail in the practical side of Ephesians, mostly in chapter 4.

<u>KEY VERSE</u>

Ephesians 4:15-16 APNT
But we should be steadfast in our love, so that [in] everything we ourselves may grow up in Christ, who is the head.
And from him the whole body is fit together and is knit together in all the joints, according to the gift that is given by measure to each member for the growth of the body, that its building up would be accomplished in love.

We are exhorted to grow up in Christ. From him the body is a unified whole and functions with him as the head. Let's take a look at the meaning of "head."

The Aramaic word for head is *risha*, and has a variety of meanings. It can mean a physical head, but when used to represent the head of other things it has four major ideas: 1) beginning or origination, 2) start or starting point in a series, 3) chief or best part, and 4) ruler or leader. Each of these definitions contributes to our understanding of what it means for Jesus Christ to be head of the body of Christ.

Colossians 1:18 APNT
And he is the head of the body, the church, for he is the beginning and the firstborn from the dead in order that he would be the first in all [things].

The first definition is "beginning." In this verse in Colossians the phrase "beginning and the firstborn" is a figure of speech, *hendiadys*, where two nouns are used but one thing meant. When we put the two words together, the phrase could be translated "firstborn leader." Jesus Christ is the eldest son in the family of God and thus he is the leader, or shows the beginning of the Father's relationship with his children. The definition of "beginning" means that there is a point of origin.

Calling Jesus Christ the "beginning and firstborn" reveals him as the starting point of the family of God. He is the eldest son and was born in a unique fashion. Every other son and daughter of God is born by God's Spirit also and is filled with the same measure that was given to Jesus Christ.

The second definition is "starting point of a series." This is similar to the first definition, but it points out that there is a series in which there is a "first." How is Jesus Christ the "first" in the body of Christ? In the previously quoted verse from Colossians 1:18, he is firstborn from the dead. He is the first of a series of people who will not be subject to death. He is also the "captain" of salvation, meaning the founder and starting point of deliverance for mankind.

Hebrews 2:10 KJV
For it became him, for whom are all things, and by whom are all things, in bringing many sons unto glory, to make the captain of their salvation perfect through sufferings.

Jesus Christ is also the author of faith or the originator of the kind of faith or believing that all believers may have now. He started this trust and reliance on God and has given it to us as part of the gift of the Spirit.

Hebrews 12:2 APNT
And we should look at Jesus, who was the initiator and finisher of our faith, who for the joy there was for him endured the cross and discounted the shame and sat down at the right hand of the throne of God.

Not only did he start the first faith and trust as a child of God, but he also completed it so that there is no need for any more faith. We have the faith of Jesus Christ—it is already ours!

Romans 3:22a APNT
But the uprightness of God is by way of the faith of Jesus Christ to everyone, even on everyone who believes in him…

The third definition of *risha* is "chief or best part." It indicates the most important or highest ranking one of a group. The Aramaic translation of Mark 12:39 talks about the "chief seats in the synagogues and the chief places at banquets" meaning the most important places. When used in architectural terms, the scriptures call Jesus Christ the head of the corner of the building.

Acts 4:11-12 KJV
This is the stone which was set at nought of you builders, which is become the head of the corner.
Neither is there salvation in any other: for there is none other name under heaven given among men, whereby we must be saved.

As we have seen before, the cornerstone of a building sets the dimensions and framework for the whole building. It sets the angles and it is the most important stone, for the rest of the building is built on it. The "head" is also the chief part of the body and sets the functioning of the various parts. Salvation is dependent on all that Jesus the Messiah did and accomplished for us and there is no life outside of him.

The last definition of *risha* is that of "ruler" or "leader." This definition is the primary usage of head when describing Jesus Christ's relationship to the Church.

Ephesians 1:22-23 APNT
And he subjected everything under his feet and he gave him who is higher than all [to be] the head of the church,
which is his body and the fullness of him who is filling all in all.

This definition is used as head or chief in the sense of rank or authority. Jesus has authority over all things of the Church. The emphasis in this verse is that HIM who is higher than all has authority.

We are held closely together as a body because of the leadership and authority of Jesus Christ. The words in Greek for "fit together" in Ephesians 4:16 are the same as the words "fitly framed together" from Ephesians 2:21 regarding the temple. This means that every part of the body is important and is also knit together. Love is the ligament that binds each joint (point of connection) together so the body can grow.

Colossians 2:19 ESV
and not holding fast to the Head, from whom the whole body, nourished and knit together through its joints and ligaments, grows with a growth that is from God.

To summarize what we have learned so far, as a physical body cannot function without a head to guide it, neither can the body of Christ function without the leadership and headship of Jesus Christ. As our big brother and the firstborn Son, he is the beginning of all of our relationships with God as the Father. He is the starting point of all deliverance and salvation. He is the chief part of the body and sets the foundation of all its dimensions. And he is the leader and head authority of all functions in the body of Christ.

Now we will look at the body of Christ as a whole unit and see that each of the individual parts cannot function without the others. The explanation of this is vividly laid out in 1 Corinthians 12:12-27 and we will study this passage in detail.

LESSON 12 ✚ JESUS CHRIST, THE HEAD OF THE BODY

1 Corinthians 12:12-14 KJV
For as the body is one, and hath many members, and all the members of that one body, being many, are one body: so also is Christ.
For by one Spirit are we all baptized into one body, whether we be Jews or Gentiles, whether we be bond or free; and have been all made to drink into one Spirit.
For the body is not one member, but many.

An individual is a member of the body. This is the great mystery, that each person has the same Spirit. But the body of Christ is not just one individual, but many. It takes all the "many" to enable it to be called a body.

1 Corinthians 12:15-18 KJV
If the foot shall say, Because I am not the hand, I am not of the body; is it therefore not of the body?
And if the ear shall say, Because I am not the eye, I am not of the body; is it therefore not of the body?
If the whole body were an eye, where were the hearing? If the whole were hearing, where were the smelling?
But now hath God set the members every one of them in the body, as it hath pleased him.

The foot and the hand are combinations of various forms of cells. The foot cannot be called a foot unless you look at the framework of bones, tissues, muscles and ligaments. So also with the eye and the ear. The unique combination of all the parts of the eye or ear allows them to do specific things.

What would we do without the ear or the eye? Even though it is unique in its function, it still requires the whole body in order to function. The sensory impulses need to be communicated back through the nervous system to the brain and thus then communicated throughout the whole body.

1 Corinthians 12:19-21 KJV
And if they were all one member, where were the body?
But now are they many members, yet but one body.
And the eye cannot say unto the hand, I have no need of thee: nor again the head to the feet, I have no need of you.

We cannot say to any part of the body of Christ, "I have no need of you." Every single function, every type of person, every group is necessary for how the Church is to live together and represent Christ. If my eye said to my hand, "I can do your job better—you don't know what is going on," then I would not be typing this manuscript. In the body of Christ, we cannot say to any other part that we do not have need of them.

1 Corinthians 12:22-24 APNT
But more, there is a necessity for those members that are thought to be weak.
And to those that we think are despised in the body, we give more honor. And for those that are modest, we make more decoration.
Now those members that we have that are honored do not require honor. For God has joined together the body and he has given more honor to the member who is least,

An example of a member of the body of Christ that is weak is a child. But the youngest child in the Church should be held in honor. Why? Because the example of the simple trusting faith of a child is the epitome of how every believer should be.

Matthew 18:2-5 KJV
And Jesus called a little child unto him, and set him in the midst of them,
And said, Verily I say unto you, Except ye be converted, and become as little children, ye shall not enter into the kingdom of heaven.
Whosoever therefore shall humble himself as this little child, the same is greatest in the kingdom of heaven.
And whoso shall receive one such little child in my name receiveth me.

The child realizes that he cannot take care of himself. We would do well to humble ourselves and have child-like faith. Being the greatest preacher or the greatest miracle worker does not determine a person's greatness in God's eyes. But humility and trust are keys to pleasing him.

The King James Version uses a phrase in 1 Corinthians 12:24 that explains how the body of Christ is supposed to fit together.

1 Corinthians 12:24-25 KJV
For our comely parts have no need: but God hath tempered the body together, having given more abundant honour to that part which lacked:
That there should be no schism in the body; but that the members should have the same care one for another.

The word "tempered" is the Greek word, *sugkerannumi,* and is a very interesting word. Its basic meaning is to mix together. Regarding the body of Christ, it means that God has caused the several parts to unite into a whole in an organic structure. The emphasis is not on the parts, but on the whole. The only other place that this word is used is in Hebrews.

Hebrews 4:2 KJV
For unto us was the gospel preached, as well as unto them: but the word preached did not profit them, not being mixed with faith in them that heard it.

Clarke's Commentary is particularly vivid in his explanation of the use of this word *sugkerannumi*:

> The word συγκεκραμενος, mixed, is peculiarly expressive; it is a metaphor taken from the nutrition of the human body by mixing the aliment taken into the stomach with the saliva and gastric juice, in consequence of which it is concocted, digested, reduced into chyle, which, absorbed by the lacteal vessels, and thrown into the blood, becomes the means of increasing and supporting the body, all the solids and fluids being thus generated; so that on this process, properly performed, depend (under God) strength, health, and life itself. Should the most nutritive aliment be received into the stomach, if not mixed with the above juices, it would be rather the means of death than of life; or, in the words of the apostle, it would not profit, because not thus mixed. Faith in the word preached, in reference to that God who sent it,[4]

The emphasis is that with the mixture, there is profit. However, Hebrews 4:2 is in the context of faith, but 1 Corinthians 12 is talking about how the body of Christ works together so that there would be no schism. All the parts are necessary! And not only that, they work together to form an organic whole that produces something more complete than the individual parts. An example would be in cooking a stir-fry meal. The chef puts in many different vegetables as well as certain seasonings, oil and flavorings. The combination of all of these produce a delicious repast that is certainly more than the individual parts.

An additional idea of this word "tempered" is that not only is there a mixing or mingling, but that there is a mutual adjustment to one another. This is vividly seen when believers of various groups work closely together and begin to depend and rely upon each other's strengths. There is an acknowledgment that the sum of the parts is greater than the individual part by itself.

---

[4] Clarke, Adam, *The New Testament of our Lord and Saviour Jesus Christ, Commentary on the Bible*, p. 709.

I believe that this word "tempered" summarizes the way that the body of Christ should work together. We each may be an individual member in the Church, but without the other members and without being tempered together with each other, the whole body will not function properly.

1 Corinthians 12:25-27 APNT
so that there would not be division in the body, but rather [that] all the members would care for one another equally,
so that when one member was hurt, all of them would suffer, and if one member was praised, all the members would be praised.
Now you are the body of Christ and members in your place.

The purpose of the tempering together is that the members would care for each other equally and appreciate all that each person offers in the body. One person by himself can only accomplish so much. Each one is necessary, but combined with other "members," he can accomplish even more.

1 Corinthians 12:27 KJV
Now ye are the body of Christ, and members in particular.

The metaphor that "ye are the body of Christ" is so powerful! When we read "ye" in the King James Version, it means you (plural), working together, loving together, living together, preaching together. We together magnify the awesome wisdom of God in placing us as particular members which make up an organic functioning unit. The picture of the body in all its various parts offers startling and thought-provoking comparisons regarding how the body of Christ functions.

Christ in you is the mystery of the one body. We each have the same measure of the Spirit. No matter where we came from or what we have done, we each have a special "particular" part in the body of Christ, the Church. Let us all get busy "growing up into him" and living in the fullness of the mystery today!

Now that we have looked at how the Church is a body and functions together let's look at some of what these functions are. You can look up these verses in your favorite translation and fill in the blanks.

Romans 12:4-8 ESV
For as in one body we have many members, and the members do not all have the same function,

so we, though many, are one body in Christ, and individually members one of another.
Having gifts that differ according to the grace given to us, let us use them: if prophecy,
in proportion to our faith;
if service, in our serving; the one who teaches, in his teaching;
the one who exhorts, in his exhortation; the one who contributes, in generosity; the one
who leads, with zeal; the one who does acts of mercy, with cheerfulness.

EXERCISE

There are seven functions listed in the previous verses. Fill in the blanks to give an example of a modern-day person or situation where you see this function in your church or fellowship group. Or if you would rather, look up someone from the book of Acts or the Epistles who demonstrates this function.

FUNCTION	PERSON WHO DEMONSTRATES
Prophesying	
Ministering	
Teaching	
Exhorting	
Giving (with generosity)	
Leading (with diligence)	
Being merciful (with cheerfulness)	

FURTHER STUDY AND DISCUSSION

1) What other functions can you think of that are important in the body of Christ?

2) How can you become more "tempered" together with members of your church?

3) What are some practical examples of "holding fast to the head"?

LESSON 13 ✠ THE POWER OF WORDS IN RELATIONSHIPS

Words can be edifying. Words can also be like poison arrows that cause death. Did you ever hear the saying, "loose lips sink ships"? Another pithy statement is, "the tongue is an unruly evil." That is from the book of James. We can move mountains with our words. We can also use words like drawn swords. We can speak words without thought and slander our best friends. But "a soft answer turneth away wrath" (Proverbs 15:1). In this lesson I want to explore the power of words for good and evil in our relationships as they are outlined in Ephesians 5:1-6:9.

First, we are told to walk in love and to imitate God as dear children and Christ as our example of love. One of the greatest ways we can show our love for someone is with our words. And some of the greatest words are ones of thanksgiving.

KEY VERSE

Ephesians 5:2-4 APNT
And walk in love, as Christ also loved us and delivered himself up for us, an offering and a sacrifice to God for a sweet smell.
But fornication and all uncleanness and greed should also especially not be named among you as is proper to holy [ones],
and neither obscenities nor words of foolishness or of reproach or of nonsense that are not necessary, but instead of these, [words of] thanksgiving.

There is an inherent power in words. With words the heavens and earth were created. The power of speech is what differentiates men from animals. With words, whole nations have been deceived and brought under the control of certain small groups of people. An example of this is how the entire population of Russia was controlled by first the czars and then the communists. With words we can bless and praise our God and Father. Ephesians goes on to exhort us to not be deceived into using "empty words" but to walk in the light.

Ephesians 5:6-9 APNT
[I say this], so that no one deceives you with empty words, for because of these [things] the wrath of God will come on the sons of disobedience.
Therefore, do not become partners with them,
for you were first of all [in] darkness, but now you are light in our Lord. Therefore, so walk as sons of light,
for the effects of the light are in all goodness and justification and truthfulness.

With words we can curse, not only our enemies, but also our friends and loved ones. This is where we have the most trouble with realizing the power of our words. What we speak about our friends and our families have the most powerful effect. Why? It is because we know them well, so we know what words will have the most impact. We easily condemn, gossip, and throw slanderous accusations—to those we love the most! How can this be? Many times, we do this without even being aware of it. Everyone has cursed someone else at some time. No one is exempt from this problem.

Ecclesiastes 7:20-22 KJV
For there is not a just man upon earth, that doeth good, and sinneth not.
Also take no heed unto all words that are spoken; lest thou hear thy servant curse thee:
For oftentimes also thine own heart knoweth that thou thyself likewise hast cursed others.

Ephesians 5 goes on to explain how to walk in the light which would dispel darkness.

Write a summary of this exhortation from verses 10-14:

_____
_____
_____
_____

The next exhortation to us is to walk "circumspectly" and to be wise.

Ephesians 5:15-21 NET
Therefore be very careful how you live – not as unwise but as wise,
taking advantage of every opportunity, because the days are evil.
For this reason do not be foolish, but be wise by understanding what the Lord's will is.
And do not get drunk with wine, which is debauchery, but be filled by the Spirit,
speaking to one another in psalms, hymns, and spiritual songs, singing and making music in your hearts to the Lord,
always giving thanks to God the Father for each other in the name of our Lord Jesus Christ,
and submitting to one another out of reverence for Christ.

What are some of the ways this passage is talking about living carefully? In what way can we use our words to be wise?

_____
_____
_____

The first thing to do in order live circumspectly is to fill our minds with the truth of the words of God. This involves listening, reading, and then keeping those verses and teaching in our thoughts. Dwell and meditate on the Word of God and that is what you will speak. The second thing to do is to be diligent to keep your heart pure. This means asking for forgiveness for times of evil speaking, for even times when we were not aware of what we were speaking. It means forgiving others for words that they have spoken against us and for breaking the power of negative words that have been sent our way, as well as ones we have sent. "Ponder the path of thy feet" from Proverbs 4:26 means to consider the areas of our lives that need correction. Is there any envy in my heart? Have I, or am I causing division of any kind? This requires a diligent seeking to root out areas of our lives that may not be pleasant to deal with. Ephesians 5 has some further insight and another crucial key.

Ephesians 5:21 APNT
And be subject to one another in the love of Christ.

In order to control the words that we speak and before we can apply that to a specific relationship, we need to understand what it means to "be subject to one another" or "submitting yourselves one to another" as the King James Version reads. We usually think of submission as something negative, but it actually has a very positive connotation. The word in both Greek and Aramaic has the idea of a proper arrangement for something. For example, I would submit to the plumber who comes to fix my clogged drain because I do not know how to fix it myself. That is a proper arrangement in that I acknowledge the plumber has more understanding and expertise in that field than I do.

When we are talking about relationships as they begin to be expressed in the rest of this section in Ephesians, then we need to remember that there are proper and godly times and forms of submission. Our relationships always have some give and take. I acknowledge that my husband has more understanding about fixing things than I do. He acknowledges and "submits" to my oversight of the finances because I have spent many years as a bookkeeper. We can see this easily with children. We would not submit ourselves to a child of four years old and expect that they would be supplying our dinner.

We will keep this in mind while reading and studying the various relationships outlined in Ephesians. First, please consider filling out the following chart and try to gain understanding directly from the verses, not your own understanding. Asking questions such as these help us to find the application in our personal lives.

VERSE	GROUP	COMMANDS	REASONS FOR COMMAND	PROMISES AND REWARDS
5:22-24	Wives			
5:25-33	Husbands			
6:1-3	Children			
6:4	Fathers			
6:5-8	Slaves (Employees)			
6:9	Masters (Employers)			

The source of our words comes from our heart. Our heart (or mind) shows what our true thoughts are and then our tongue brings those out. If our minds are filled with spiritual words, then that is what we will speak. The gospel of John is full of passages regarding words and believing Jesus' words. Jesus showed that his words came from the Father and thus were spiritual words. Those words then brought life to people who believed them.

John 6:63 KJV
It is the spirit that quickeneth; the flesh profiteth nothing: the words that I speak unto you, they are spirit, and they are life.

The best source of all words is the Spirit. Spiritual words, such as those from the Word of God, bring life. This is very easy to see when we are standing in the pulpit preaching the gospel or when witnessing to people. But what about after the service is over? Or after the time of fellowship? What do we speak when we are at home with our families? What do we speak in our workplaces about our employers?

Let us seek to use the words we speak to bring health and life and to be spiritual words of truth in ALL our relationships. Let us speak the words of life and endeavor to root out the impurities in our hearts. Let us walk in love, in light and circumspectly. Let us use our words to pray for others and to give thanks!

FURTHER STUDY AND DISCUSSION

1. What are four characteristics of a good workman from Ephesians 6:5-8?

2. What does it mean to "bring up a child in the nurture and admonition of the Lord"?

3. Consider other relationships where words are important.

LESSON 14 ⹎ STANDING TOGETHER AS ONE

We have studied a lot about the mystery revealed in the book of Ephesians. What God did by giving the full measure of the gift of the Spirit to each believer completely defeated the plans of the Evil One.

1 Corinthians 2:7-8 KJV
But we speak the wisdom of God in a mystery, even the hidden wisdom, which God ordained before the world unto our glory:
Which none of the princes of this world knew: for had they known it, they would not have crucified the Lord of glory.

The wisdom of God foiled the strategy of the prince of this world, the Evil One, when God raised Jesus from the dead. If he had known God's plan, he never would have orchestrated the crucifixion.

It is now available for us to have the same measure of the gift of the Spirit as Christ. We can walk with the same power and operate all the manifestations of that gift to defeat the influences of the Devil. It is Christ in us, the hope of glory. So, wherever there is a believer that has this power, it is as though Christ is walking there. Every believer now has the same authority over sickness, sin, the environment, and everything that Christ has authority over!

The main tool of the Adversary is the sin nature and resulting sins, which issue finally in death. As the mystery was revealed, full identification with Christ is defined. A believer died with Christ and thus is dead to trespasses and sins. They no longer have dominion over him. He was raised with Christ, quickened together with him, ascended with him and seated with him in the heavenlies. Every believer will be raised with him in glory. The ultimate weapon, death, is no longer to be feared.

Hebrews 2:14-15 APNT
For because the sons share in flesh and blood, he also in the same manner shared of the same, that by his death he would put a stop to him who held the authority of death, who is Satan,
and would release those who by fear of death were subjected to bondage all their lives.

We have power in the full measure of Christ. We have the unity of the Spirit that cancels all division and we have the dominion over our sin nature and death. By God's wisdom, the Devil's best tools were totally defeated.

If that was not enough, God had hidden the great mystery by his wisdom and gradually revealed it to the first century believers. This mystery as it was made known, showed the unity which men had together. All of the separations and divisions (one of the Adversary's most effective tools to "steal, kill and destroy") were broken down. The main separation that was broken down was the one between Israel, the people of God, and the Gentiles, all the other nations. However, other conflicts were also abolished.

Galatians 3:28 ESV
There is neither Jew nor Greek, there is neither slave nor free, there is no male and female, for you are all one in Christ Jesus.

This unity was made possible again by the Spirit born within each believer. So, not only did they have the power of Christ, but all divisions were made of none effect. Had the prince of the world known this, he never would have crucified Jesus Christ!

The last section of Ephesians (6:10-18) is about the armor of God and I have written a book, *The Armor of Victory,* covering the analogy of the soldier. But before we zero in on the pieces of the armor, let's take a look at the key word, "stand."

KEY VERSE

Ephesians 6:10-14 APNT
From now on, my brothers, be strong in our Lord and in the immensity of his power and put on the whole armor of God, so that you may be able to stand against the tactics of the Accuser,
because your struggle is not with flesh and blood, but with rulers and with authorities and with the possessors of this dark world and with the evil spirits that are under heaven.
Because of this, put on the whole armor of God, so that you will be able to engage the Evil [one] and, being prepared in everything, you will stand firm.
Therefore, stand and....

We are told to "stand against the tactics of the Accuser" and "stand firm" and "therefore, stand." Our strength and victory are in the Lord and in the immensity of his power. With the whole armor of God, we are prepared in everything so we CAN stand firm. Remember in Lesson 2 we learned about the Greek work *en*, which means "in, remaining in"? Throughout the epistles, although there are two different Greek words for "stand" they each are used with the preposition *en*. Take the time to fill in the following chart.

VERSES FROM APNT	"IN" WHAT?
Romans 5:2 by whom we were brought by faith to this grace in which we stand and boast in the hope of the glory of God.	
1 Corinthians 15:1 Now I make known to you, my brothers, the gospel that I preached to you and [that] you received and in which you stand	
1 Corinthians 16:13 Watch and stand in the faith. Act mature. Be strong.	
Philippians 1:27 Conduct yourselves as is becoming to the gospel of Christ, so that if I come, I may see you and if I am distant, I may hear about you, that you are standing in one spirit and in one soul and [that] you are conquering together in the faith of the gospel.	
Philippians 4:1 From now on, my beloved and dear brothers, my joy and my crown, so stand fast in our Lord, my beloved.	
Colossians 4:12 Epaphras greets you, who is one of you, a servant of Christ, laboring at all times for you in prayer, that you would stand, mature [ones] and complete [ones] in all the will of God.	

Here are some definitions for "to stand" from both Greek and Aramaic that are particularly apropos for this section:

1. Make firm, establish
2. Uphold or sustain the authority or force of anything
3. Stand immovable, stand firm
4. Continue safe and sound, stand unharmed, stand ready or prepared
5. Stand firm, persevere, persist

Go back to the filled-in chart and repeat these definitions in regard to what we stand in. This is an individual stand, but it is also a collective one. The verbs for standing in Ephesians 6 are all plural. We need to stand together and it is as we help each other with putting on the armor, we will become "mature ones" in the will of God. It is truly his will that we be "more than conquerors."

Now, I want to zero in on the illustration of the family and how the pieces of the armor can be used to show us how to stand together as one. We have the unity of the Spirit; now we need to stand in it with each other.

Ephesians 6:14-17 APNT
Therefore, stand and gird up your waist with truthfulness and put on the breastplate of justification
and bind [as a sandal] on your feet the goodness of the gospel of peace.
And with these, take to you the shield of faith, by which you will be empowered with strength to quench all the fiery arrows of the Evil [One].
And set on [your head] the helmet of redemption and take hold of the sword of the Spirit, which is the word of God.

Here are the pieces of the armor and what they represent:

Girdle	God's faithfulness to his Word
Breastplate	Justification and righteousness
Sandals	Gospel of the mystery, every person has a place
Shield	Faith in the name of Jesus Christ
Helmet	Hope of redemption
Sword	The living Word of God

The six pieces of the armor are listed in a particular order in Ephesians, but I want to deviate from that and think about how we would put these pieces on if we were getting dressed in regular clothes. The word for "put on" in verse 14 can be translated, "get dressed." Now what is the order in which we would get dressed?

First, we need undergarments and clothes to cover the body. That means the breastplate comes first. The application of how to stand together is that we each as individuals must identify with the righteousness given by Christ. We have to believe that of ourselves, but also of each other. If everyone is righteous, then divisions, such as between young and old, do not matter anymore. If we live in a household and family, it is important to be especially good to each other and that means we believe that each person is justified and free from blame.

Galatians 6:10 KJV
As we have therefore opportunity, let us do good unto all men, especially unto them who are of the household of faith.

The second piece that would be put on would be the belt of truth. That piece of the armor represents that God is always faithful to his Word and his promises will always come to pass. This is to anchor our clothes together and be the place where we hang the sword next. The sword is the Word of God as it is revealed by the Spirit. In order to stand together as a family, we must be firmly girded with the truth of the written Word and hang our practice of how we relate to each other on that truth. An example would be a believer who has been hurt by a fellowship or church and now does not want to participate in anything. We can teach the principles of forgiveness from the Bible and then offer our hands of acceptance and love in a practical way to draw them back into relationship.

Hebrews 10:22-25 NLT
let us go right into the presence of God with sincere hearts fully trusting him. For our guilty consciences have been sprinkled with Christ's blood to make us clean [breastplate], and our bodies have been washed with pure water.
Let us hold tightly without wavering to the hope we affirm, for God can be trusted to keep his promise.
Let us think of ways to motivate one another to acts of love and good works.
And let us not neglect our meeting together, as some people do, but encourage one another, especially now that the day of his return is drawing near.

Can you think of another example how these two pieces of the armor (belt and sword) would apply in a family or church situation?

_____

_____

_____

_____

The next piece of clothing to put on would be the sandals or shoes. The gospel of the mystery which brings peace is that every believer has a place in the body of Christ. Therefore, no pride or jealousy or manipulation is needed; instead, there is a firm footing to practically stand next to one another. Some divisions which do occur in the household are between clergy and laymen, and between male and female. Clergy or ministers need to be servants first and are not to lord over those in their "family." Men are also to be nurturing and not bossy, but women are also not supposed to be manipulative or controlling either.

1 Peter 5:1-3 ESV
So I exhort the elders among you, as a fellow elder and a witness of the sufferings of
Christ, as well as a partaker in the glory that is going to be revealed:
shepherd the flock of God that is among you, exercising oversight, not under
compulsion, but willingly, as God would have you; not for shameful gain, but eagerly;
not domineering over those in your charge, but being examples to the flock.

Think of another example of how this piece of armor is applied in a church family. You could read the context of 1 Peter 5 to see some keys.

_____
_____
_____
_____

The next piece of the armor to put on is the helmet. This is the helmet of redemption where we have been given freedom instead of slavery, life instead of death, deliverance instead of bondage. It is also called the "helmet of the hope of salvation." A hat or headgear would protect the head from all the outward elements. It is particularly necessary in a cold climate when the temperatures dip below freezing! The application in a family is that we need to look out for each other and help encourage the use of this headgear when a person is struggling with something like addictions or depression. We do not wrestle against people, but against the wicked spirits from on high, who greatly delight in putting people in bondage. Instead of judgment and criticism, we need to offer help to each other to be delivered from any bondage.

The last piece of clothing to put on would be to take up the shield of faith. This is the authority we have in Christ to use his name and to quench the fiery darts of the Evil One. This is also what we use to help protect each other in the family when someone needs to be supported. This is not our faith; it is the faith that resides in the power of Jesus Christ. We can lock our shields together to present an impenetrable front.

Can you think of a situation where there was a need for another's shield?

_____
_____
_____

Here is the conclusion of how we stand together as one. We have to be fully dressed with the armor of God, standing in grace, in the gospel, in the faith, in the Lord, in one Spirit. We have the complete victory already in Christ Jesus. Therefore, stand…

FURTHER STUDY AND DISCUSSION

1) Has any piece of the armor of God been battered in your spiritual battles and if so, which piece? How can that area be strengthened?

2) How is prayer (Ephesians 6:18) a vital part of putting on the armor? How is it related to the armor?

3) Who was Tychicus and why was he called "a faithful minister in the Lord"?

ARAMAIC PESHITTA NEW TESTAMENT TRANSLATION—EPHESIANS

Chapter 1

1   Paul, an apostle of Jesus Christ, by the will of God, to those who are in Ephesus, holy [ones] and faithful [ones] in Jesus Christ:

2   Peace [be] with you and grace from God our Father and from our Lord Jesus Christ.

3   Blessed be God, the Father of our Lord Jesus Christ, who has blessed us with all spiritual blessings[1] in heaven in Christ,

4   even as he chose us beforehand in him, from before the foundations of the world, that we should be holy [ones] and without blemish before him. And in love, he marked us out beforehand[2] for himself

5   and he adopted us in Jesus Christ, as was pleasing to his will,

6   that the [as]glory of his grace would be glorified,[3] which he has poured on us by way of his beloved [one],

7   in whom we have redemption and remission of sins by his blood, according to the [as]wealth of his grace,

8   which he caused to abound in us with all wisdom and with all[4] understanding.

9   And he made known to us the [as]mystery of his will that he had determined beforehand to accomplish in him,

10 in the administration of the fullness of times, that everything that is in heaven and in earth should be made new again in Christ.

11 And **we** were chosen in him, even as he marked us out beforehand[5] and he desired, he who performs everything according to the [as]purpose of his will,

12 that **we**, those who first trusted in Christ, should be for the [as]esteem of his magnificence.

---

[1] Same root: *blessed, blessings*

[2] Repeat *beforehand*, also vs. 9, 11

[3] Same root: *glory, glorified*; fig: antiptosis, 6x, vs. 6-14, "his glorious grace," "his rich grace," "his secret purpose," "his intended will," "his honorable glory," "his glorious honor"

[4] Repeat *with all*; Var (WSLM): add 'spiritual'

[5] Repeat *marked us out beforehand* from v. 4; word picture: *marked out* is "to engrave as a tattoo"

13 In him also, ^{ac}**you** heard the ^{an}word of truthfulness, which is
the gospel of your life, and in him, you believed and you were
sealed with the Holy Spirit that was promised,

14 which is the guarantee of our inheritance to the redemption of
those who have life and to the ^{as}glory of his honor.

15 Because of this, *behold, **I** also, since I heard of your faith that
is in our Lord Jesus Christ and your love that is toward the holy
[ones],

16 have not ceased to give thanks for you and to remember you in
my prayers,

17 that the God of our Lord Jesus Christ, the ^{an}Father of glory,
would give you the Spirit of wisdom and of revelation in his
knowledge[1]

18 and [that] the ^meyes of your hearts would be enlightened, so
that you would know what is the hope of his calling and what is
the ^{an}wealth of the glory of his inheritance in the holy [ones]

19 and what is the ^{an}abundance of the greatness of his power in
us, in those who believe, according to the ^{an}working of the might
of his power.

20 [This is] he who worked in Christ and raised him from the
dead and seated him at his right hand in heaven,

21 higher than all rulers ^pand authorities and powers and lordships
and higher than every name that is named, not only in this world,
but in the coming [one] also.

22 And **HE SUBJECTED EVERYTHING UNDER HIS** ^{sy}**FEET** and he
gave him who is higher than all [to be] the ^hhead of the church,

23 ^{me}which is his body and the fullness of him who is filling all in
all.[2]

Chapter 2

1 And ^e[God is filling] even you who were dead in your sins and
in your transgressions,

2 in which you had walked previously, according to the
worldliness of this world [3] and according to the will of the chief
authority of the air and of that[4] spirit that operates in the sons of
disobedience.

---

[1] Or "by the knowledge of him"

[2] Repeat *all*; same root: *fullness, filling*

[3] Same root: *worldliness, world*; repeat *previously*, vs. 3, 10, 11

[4] Var (WSLM): omit *that*

3   **We** also were occupied in those deeds previously, in the desires of our [sy]flesh, and we were doing the will of our [sy]flesh and of our mind and we were the sons of wrath [as] fully as the rest.

4   But God, who is rich in his mercies, because of his great love [with] which he loved us, [1]

5   while we were dead in our sins, gave us life with Christ and, by his grace, redeemed us

6   [p]and raised us with him and seated us with him in heaven in Jesus Christ,

7   so that he could show to the ages that are coming the [as]greatness of the wealth of his grace and his goodness that is to us in Jesus Christ.

8   For by his grace we were redeemed by faith [pa]and this was not from yourselves, but is the gift of God,

9   not from works, so that no one would boast.

10 For we [are] his own creation, who are created in Jesus Christ for good works, those [e][works] which God prepared previously that we should walk in.

11 Because of this, remember that [ac]you were previously Gentiles in the [sy]flesh and you were called the [m]uncircumcision by that which is called the [m]circumcision and is [pr]the work of the hands in the flesh.

12 And at that time, you were without Christ [p]and you were aliens from the customs of Israel and you were strangers to the covenant of the promise and you were without hope and without[2] God in the world.

13 But now, in Jesus Christ, **you** who previously [3]were far have become near by the [mt]blood of Christ.

14 [al]For [me]he was our peace treaty, who made the two of them one and has broken down the [h]wall that stood in the middle[4]

15 and the conflict, by his flesh. And he brought to an end the law of commandments with its commandments,[5] so that [from] the two of them he would create in himself one [h]new man, and he made a peace treaty.

---

[1] Same root: *love, loved*; repeat *us* as suffix, vs. 4-6

[2] Repeat *without*, 3x

[3] Repeat *previously* from vs. 10, 11

[4] Fig: hypocatastasis, *wall* stands for the law, comparing it to the wall separating the Jews and Gentiles in the temple

[5] Repeat *commandments*

16 And he reconciled the two of them with God in one [h]body and, by his [mt]cross, he destroyed the conflict.

17 And he came [and] **HE DECLARED PEACE TO YOU, [BOTH] THE FAR AND THE NEAR,**

18 because in him we both have access in one spirit to the Father.

19 From now on, you are neither strangers nor foreigners, but citizens who are holy [ones] and [of] the household of God.

20 [al]And you are built on the foundation of the apostles and of the prophets and Jesus Christ is the head of the corner of the building.[1]

21 And in him the whole building is fit together and is growing into a holy temple in the LORD,

22 while **you** also are built in him for a dwelling of God spiritually.

Chapter 3

1 Because of this, **I**, Paul, am a prisoner of Jesus Christ for you Gentiles,

2 even as you have heard of the administration of the grace of God that was given to me among you,

3 that by revelation the mystery was made known to me [pa](as I have written to you in few [words],

4 so that you may be able, while you are reading, to understand my knowledge that is in the mystery of Christ),

5 which in other generations was not made known to men, as that which now has been revealed to his holy apostles and to his prophets spiritually,

6 that the Gentiles should be his heirs and participants of his [h]body and of [2] the promise that was given in him, by way of the gospel,

7 [pa]of which **I** became a minister according to the gift of the grace of God that was given to me by the working of his power.

8 To me, [t]who am the least of all the holy [ones], this grace was given, that I should declare among the Gentiles the wealth of Christ that is untraceable

9 and [that] I should bring light to everyone what is the administration of the mystery that was hidden from the ages in God, who created all [things],

---

[1] Same root: *built, building*, vs. 20-22; lit: **he** is the head of the corner of the building, Jesus Christ

[2] Var (WS): 'in' or 'by'

10 so that by way of the church, the extraordinary[1] wisdom of God would be made known to the rulers and to the authorities that are in heaven,

11 which e[wisdom] he had prepared from the ages and has performed in Jesus Christ our Lord,

12 in whom we have heboldness and access in the confidence of his faith.

13 Because of this,[2] I am petitioning that I will not be weary in my trials that are for you, because this is your glory,

14 and prI bow my knees to the Father of our Lord Jesus Christ,

15 from whom all the family which is in heaven and on earth is named,

16 that he would allow[3] you, according to the anwealth of his glory, to be strengthened with power by his Spirit, that in your inner man

17 Christ would dwell in faith and in your hearts in love, as your hroot and your hfoundation becomes strong,

18 that you would be able to understand with all the holy [ones] what is the height pand depth and length and breadth

19 and would know the asgreatness of the knowledge[4] of the love of Christ and would be filled with all the fullness[5] of God.

20 beNow to him who is able, by surpassing power, to do even more for us than what we ask and think, according to his power that is performed in us,

21 to him [be] glory in his church by Jesus Christ in all generations, forever and ever. Amen.

Chapter 4

1 I, therefore, a prisoner in our Lord, beg you that you should walk as is proper for the calling that you were called,[6]

2 with all humbleness of mind and quietness and long-suffering. And hold up one another in love

---

[1] Lit: full of distinctions

[2] Repeat *because of this* from v. 1, ties the passage to a new context; vs. 1-12 could also be a long parenthesis.

[3] Lit: give

[4] Var (WS): omit *of the knowledge*; same root: *know, knowledge*

[5] Same root: *filled, fullness*

[6] Same root: *calling, called*, also v. 4

3   and be diligent to keep the alliance of the Spirit with the
[m]girdle of peace,[1]

4   so that you will be in one body and by one Spirit, even as you
are called in one hope of your calling.

5   For [there] is one LORD and one faith and one baptism

6   and one God, the Father of all and above all and by all and in
us all.[2]

7   Now to each one of us is given grace according to the measure
of the gift of Christ.

8   Because of this, it is said, **HE ASCENDED TO THE HEIGHT AND
CAPTURED CAPTIVITY AND GAVE GIFTS[3] TO MEN.**

9   [pa](Now what is it that he ascended, unless he had also first
descended to the depths of the earth?

10 He who descended is he who also ascended higher than all the
heaven, that he would complete all.)

11 And he gave some apostles and some prophets and some
evangelists and some pastors and some[4] teachers,

12 for the maturity of the holy [ones], for the work of the
ministry, for the building up of the [h]body of Christ,

13 until we all become one in the faith and in the knowledge of
the Son of God and one mature man, in the [an]measure of the
standing of the fullness of Christ.[5]

14 And we should not be babies, who are shaken and blown about
by every wind[6] of the deceitful teachings of men, who in their
craftiness are plotting to deceive.

15 But we should be steadfast in our love, so that [in] everything
of ours [al]we may grow up in Christ, who is the head.

16 And from him the whole body is fit together and is knit
together in all the joints, according to the gift that is given by
measure to each member for the growth of the body, that its
building up would be accomplished in love.

---

[1] Fig: metonymy, the Spirit is the bond or tie that brings peace

[2] Repeat *one, all*, vs. 5, 6

[3] Same root: *capture, captivity* and *gave, gifts*

[4] Repeat *and some*

[5] Fig: antimeria, with 2 nouns, could be translated "the full, high,
measure", or with 1 noun, it would be "the measure of the full standing"

[6] Fig: antiprosopaeia, comparing babies to ships blown about in a storm

17 Now *this I say and I bear witness in the LORD, that from now on you should not walk as the rest of the Gentiles, who walk in the emptiness[1] of their mind[s]

18 ᵖand are dark in their thoughts and are strangers from the life of God, because there is no knowledge in them and because of the blindness of their heart[s],

19 those who have cut off their hope and have surrendered themselves to perversion and to the ᵃⁿwork of all uncleanness[2] in their greediness.

20 But **you** did not so learn about Christ,

21 ᵖᵃif truly you have heard him and by him you have learned, as truthfulness is in Jesus.

22 But ᵉ[you have learned] that you should strip off your former ways of life, that ʰold man who was corrupted by the ᵃⁿlusts of deceit,

23 and you should be renewed by the Spirit, that is, your minds.

24 And you should put on the ʰnew man, who was created by God by justification and by the ᵃⁿpardoning of truthfulness.

25 Because of this, strip off [3] lying and **SPEAK [WITH] TRUTHFULNESS, EACH ONE WITH HIS NEIGHBOR,** for ᵐᵉwe are members of one another.

26 **BE ANGRY AND DO NOT SIN** and the sun should not go down on your anger.[4]

27 And do not give place[5] to the ACCUSER.

28 And he who was stealing should no longer steal,[6] but he should work with his ˢʸhands and should do good [things], so that he may have to give to him who has need.

29 No hateful word should come out of your mouth, but that which is pleasing and useful for building up, so that it may give grace to those who hear.

30 And you should not grieve the sanctified Spirit of God, by whom you were sealed until the ˢʸday of redemption.

31 All bitterness ᵖand wrath and anger and contention and reviling should be taken away from you with all wickedness.

---

[1] Or "worthlessness"

[2] Fig: antimeria, could be translated "unclean practice"

[3] Repeat *strip off* from v. 22

[4] Same root: *angry, anger*

[5] Or "opportunity"

[6] Repeat forms of *steal*

32   And be kind to one another [p]and merciful and be forgiving to one another, as God in Christ forgave [ac]us.

Chapter 5
1   Therefore, imitate God as beloved sons.
2   And walk in love, as Christ also loved[1] us and delivered himself up for us, an [he]offering and a sacrifice to God for a sweet smell.
3   But fornication and all uncleanness and greed should also especially not be named[2] among you as is proper to holy [ones],
4   and neither obscenities nor words of foolishness or of reproach or[3] of nonsense that are not necessary, but instead of these, [e][words of] thanksgiving.
5   But this you should know, that everyone who is a fornicator or unclean or greedy, who is an idol worshipper, does not have an inheritance in the kingdom of Christ and of God.
6   [e][I say this], so that no one deceives you with empty words, for because of these [things] the [c]wrath of God will come on the sons of disobedience.[4]
7   Therefore, do not become partners with them,
8   [al]for you were first of all [in] darkness, but now [me]you are light in our Lord. Therefore, so walk as sons of light,
9   for the [m]effects[5] of the light are in all goodness [p]and justification and truthfulness.[6]
10   And determine what is pleasing before our Lord
11   and do not fellowship with the works of darkness that have no [e][good] [m]effects, but reprove them,
12   for what they do in secret is abominable even to speak,
13   for everything is exposed and is revealed by the light and everything that reveals[7] is light.
14   Because of this, it is said, "Awake, sleeper, and rise up from the dead, and Christ will enlighten you."

---

[1] Same root: *love, loved*

[2] Fig: polyptoton, lit: naming, be not named

[3] Repeat *nor, or*, also v. 5

[4] Or "disobedient [ones]"

[5] Lit: fruit, also v. 11

[6] Fig: hendiatris, meaning "true, just, goodness"

[7] Repeat forms of *revealed* and *light*

15 Therefore, see how you should walk accurately, not as fools, but as wise [ones]

16 who buy their opportunity,[1] because the days are evil.

17 Because of this, do not be **stupid**, but understand what is the will of God.

18 And do not be drunk with wine, in which is excess, but be filled with the Spirit,

19 and speak among yourselves with psalms and with hymns. And sing in your hearts to the LORD with songs of the Spirit.

20 And give thanks always for everyone in the name of our Lord Jesus Christ to God the Father.

21 And be subject[2] to one another in the love of Christ.

22 Wives, be subject to your husbands as to our Lord,

23 because the [me]man is the head of the wife, as also [me]Christ is the head of the church and he is the life-giver of the [h]body.

24 But even as the church is subject to Christ, so also wives [e][should be subject] to their husbands in everything.

25 Men, love your wives [al]as also Christ loved his church and delivered himself up for it,

26 to make it holy and to cleanse it by the washing of [m]water and by the word

27 and to establish the church for himself, being glorious and having no spot and no wrinkle and nothing like these, but rather to be holy [and] without blemish.

28 So it is right for men to love their wives as their [own] bodies, for he who loves his wife loves himself,

29 for no one ever hates[3] his body, but nourishes it and cares for his own [e][body]. [It is] even as Christ [e][nourishes and cares] for his church,[4]

30 because [me]we are members of his body, and we are of his flesh and of his bones.

31 Because of this, **A MAN SHOULD LEAVE HIS FATHER [p]AND HIS MOTHER AND SHOULD BE JOINED TO HIS WIFE AND THE TWO OF THEM SHOULD BECOME ONE [sy]FLESH.**

32 This mystery is great, but **I** am speaking about Christ and about[1] his church.

---

[1] Cf Grk: **kairos**; we would say "make the best use of your time."

[2] Repeat *be subject*, vs. 21-24

[3] Lit: a man never hates

[4] Var (WSLM): 'the church'

33 Nevertheless, **you** also, each and every one of you, should so have compassion for his wife as for himself and the wife should have respect for her husband.

Chapter 6

1   Children, obey your parents in our Lord, for this [is] upright.

2   And this is the first commandment that has a promise: **HONOR YOUR FATHER AND YOUR MOTHER,**

3   THAT IT MAY BE WELL FOR YOU AND YOUR LIFE MAY BE LONG ON THE EARTH.

4   Parents, do not anger your children, but rear them in the instruction and in[2] the teaching of our Lord.

5   Servants, be obedient to your masters that are in the [sy]flesh, with reverence and with [h]trembling and with simplicity of heart, as to Christ,

6   not with what is seen by the eye[3] as if you were pleasing men, but [s]as servants of Christ, who are doing the will of God.

7   And minister to them from your whole life in love, as to our Lord, and not as to men,

8   knowing that what someone does that is good will be rewarded from our Lord, whether he is a servant or a free man.

9   Also, **you** masters, so serve your servants.[4] Forgive them an error,[5] because you also know that your own Master is in heaven and there is no respect of persons with him.

10   From now on, my brothers, be strong in our Lord and in the [as]immensity of his power

11   [al]and put on the whole armor of God, so that you may be able to stand against the tactics of the Accuser,

12   because your struggle is not with [sy]flesh and blood, but with rulers [p]and with authorities and with the possessors of this dark world and with the evil spirits that are under heaven.[6]

13   Because of this, put on the whole armor of God, so that you will be able to engage the Evil [one] and, being prepared in everything, you will stand firm.

---

[1] Repeat *about*

[2] Repeat *in*

[3] Lit: the sight of the eye

[4] Same root: *serve, servants*

[5] Var (W): *errors* (pl)

[6] Repeat *and with*

14 Therefore, stand[1] and **GIRD UP YOUR WAIST WITH TRUTH-FULNESS** and **PUT ON THE BREASTPLATE OF JUSTIFICATION**
15 and **BIND [AS A SANDAL] ON YOUR FEET THE GOODNESS OF THE GOSPEL OF PEACE.**
16 And with these, take to you the ᵐshield of faith,[2] by which you will be empowered with strength to quench all the fiery ʰarrows of the Evil [one].
17 And **SET ON [YOUR HEAD] THE HELMET OF REDEMPTION** and take hold of the ᵐsword of the Spirit, which is the word of God.
18 And with all prayers and with all petitions, pray at all times spiritually, and in prayer, be watchful in every season, praying continually and interceding for all[3] the holy [ones],
19 [and] also for me, that the word may be given to me in the ᵖʳopening of my mouth, that I would boldly preach the mystery of the gospel,
20 for which ᵐᵉI am its ambassador in chains, that with frankness I may speak, as I ought to speak[4] it.
21 Now that you also may know about me[5] and what I am doing, *behold, Tychicus, a beloved brother and faithful minister in our Lord, will make known ᵉ[these things] to you,
22 whom I sent to you especially for this,[6] that you would know how [it is] with me[7] and [that] he would comfort your hearts.
23 ᵇᵉPeace [be] with our brothers and love with faith, from God the Father and from our Lord Jesus Christ.
24 Grace [be] with all those who love our Lord Jesus Christ without corruption. Amen.

---

[1] Repeat *stand* as next word from v. 13

[2] Var (S): 'hope of faith'

[3] Repeat *all*, 5x; same root: *pray, prayer*

[4] Repeat *speak*

[5] Lit: what to me

[6] Lit: for it, for this

[7] Lit: how to me

A COMPARISON OF EPHESIANS AND COLOSSIANS

PARALLELS	EPHESIANS	COLOSSIANS
Addressed to the faithful	1:1	1:2
Holy and without blame	1:4	1:22
Redemption and forgiveness of sins	1:7	1:14
Reconcile all things in heaven and earth	1:10	1:20
Prayer of thanks	1:15-16	1:3-4
Prayer for God to give wisdom	1:17	1:9
Glorious inheritance	1:18	1:27
Raised Christ from dead	1:19-20	2:12
Christ, head of the Church	1:21-23	1:16-20
Made alive (quickened)	2:1, 5	2:13
Children of disobedience	2:2-3	3:6
Raised together	2:6	2:12
Aliens reconciled, made peace	2:12	1:21-22
Abolished enmity of the law	2:15	2:14
Mystery of Christ, Paul a minister	3:1-7	1:23-26
Administration of the mystery	3:8-9	1:15-18
Walk worthy	4:1	1:10
Humility, meekness, longsuffering	4:2	3:12
Grow up into head, body joined together	4:15-16	2:19
Put off old man, put on new	4:22-24	3:9-10
No immorality	5:3-6	3:5-9

A COMPARISON OF EPHESIANS AND COLOSSIANS

Walk wisely, redeem time	5:15	4:5
Speak psalms, hymns and give thanks	5:19-20	3:16-17
Exhortations to wives	5:22-24	3:18
Exhortations to husbands	5:25-33	3:19
Exhortations to children	6:1-3	3:20
Exhortations to fathers	6:4	3:21
Exhortations to slaves	6:5-8	3:22-25
Exhortations to masters	6:9	4:1
Persist in prayer	6:18-20	4:2-4
Tychicus sent to them	6:21-22	4:7-8

BIBLIOGRAPHY

Brown, Francis, S.R. Driver, Charles A. Briggs, eds. *The New Brown-Driver-Briggs-Gesenius Hebrew and English Lexicon.* Christian Copyrights, Inc., 1983.

Bullinger, E. W. *A Critical Lexicon and Concordance to the English and Greek New Testament.* Grand Rapids, Michigan: Zondervan Publishing House, 1975.

Bullinger, E.W. *Figures of Speech Used in the Bible.* Grand Rapids, Michigan: Baker Book House, 1968.

Harris, R. Laird, Gleason L. Archer, Jr., Bruce K. Waltke, eds. *Theological Wordbook of the Old Testament* 2 volumes. Chicago, Illinois: Moody Press, 1980.

Jennings, William. *Lexicon to the Syriac New Testament.* London: Oxford University Press, 1926.

Murdock, James, trans. *The New Testament.* New York: Stanford and Swords, 1852.

Nave, Orville J. *The New Nave's Topical Bible.* Grand Rapids, Michigan: Zondervan Publishing House, 1969.

Ryken, Leland, ed. *Dictionary of Biblical Imagery.* Downers Grove, Illinois: Inter-Varsity Press, 1998.

Smith, J. Payne. *A Compendious Syriac Dictionary*. London: Oxford at the Clarendon Press, 1967.

Webster, Noah. *Noah Webster's First Edition of an American Dictionary of the English Language.* San Francisco: Foundation for American Christian Education, 1967.

REFERENCES ON EPHESIANS

Hughes, R. Kent. *Ephesians: The Mystery of the Body of Christ.* Wheaton, Illinois: Crossway, 1990.

Jensen, Irving L. *Ephesians: A Self-Study Guide.* Chicago: Moody Press, 1973.

McGee, J. Vernon. *Ephesians.* Pasadena, California: Thru the Bible Books, 1977.

BIBLIOGRAPHY

Moule, H.C.G. *Studies in Ephesians.* Grand Rapids, Michigan: Kregel Publications,

Nee, Watchman. *Site, Walk, Stand.* Carol Stream, Illinois: Tyndale House Publishers, 1977.

Paxson, Ruth. *The Wealth, Walk and Warfare of the Christian.* Westwood, New Jersey: Fleming H. Revell Company, 1936.

The Teacher's Outline and Study Bible: Ephesians. Chattanooga, Tennessee: Leadership Ministries Worldwide, 1994.

Wade, Peter. *I'm Excited About Ephesians.* Positive Word Ministries, 2017.

Wadge, Rik B. *Discovering the Jewish Roots of the Letter to the Ephesians,* Jewish Roots Publishing, 2015.

Welch, Charles H. *The Testimony of the Lord's Prisoner.* London: The Berean Publishing Trust, 1931.

Welch, Charles H. *In Heavenly Place.* London: The Berean Publishing Trust, 1968.

ABOUT THE AUTHOR

Janet Magiera is an ordained minister and the founder of Light of the Word Ministry, a ministry dedicated to teaching and making known the understanding of the Aramaic language, figures of speech and customs of the Bible. In 1979, under the tutelage of a student of Dr. George M. Lamsa, Jan began pursuing a course of study of the Aramaic Peshitta New Testament. For over 40 years, she has taught in Bible fellowships and churches in the United States and other countries, using insight from her understanding of the biblical languages. Many articles and teachings of interest are available on the Light of the Word Ministry website, www.lightofword.org.

In 1990, Jan began compiling a database of the Aramaic Peshitta New Testament. As computer technology increased over the years, she expanded and developed the database to generate a series of research tools to study the New Testament. The entire database originally was developed as a software module for BibleWorks, which is not being published anymore. The database is now available to search online at www.aramaicdb.lightofword.org. The *Aramaic Peshitta New Testament Translation* was the first book published in 2006 of a complete *Aramaic Peshitta New Testament Library*. The library includes an interlinear, lexicon, concordance, and parallel translations. There is an app of the Aramaic translation on both Apple and GooglePlay, as well as various electronic versions of her books and the translations.

Jan has also authored several topical books on biblical subjects: *Enriched in Everything* on giving, *Members in Particular* on the body of Christ, and *The Armor of Victory* on the armor of God, *The Fence of Salvation* on Hebrew and Aramaic word pictures. Her latest publication, *The Coming of the Son of Man,* is about the sequence of events of the end times.

She and her husband Glen currently live in San Diego, California. Together they have four children and eleven grandchildren.

CPSIA information can be obtained
at www.ICGtesting.com
Printed in the USA
FSHW020217291221
87029FS

9 781732 662513